GUIDANCE MONOGRAPH SERIES

Sʜᴇʟʟᴇʏ C. Sᴛᴏɴᴇ

Bʀᴜᴄᴇ Sʜᴇʀᴛᴢᴇʀ

Editors

GUIDANCE MONOGRAPH SERIES

The general purpose of Houghton Mifflin's Guidance Monograph Series is to provide high quality coverage of topics which are of abiding importance in contemporary counseling and guidance practice. In a rapidly expanding field of endeavor, change and innovation are inevitably present. A trend accompanying such growth is greater and greater specialization. Specialization results in an increased demand for materials which reflect current modifications in guidance practice while simultaneously treating the field in greater depth and detail than commonly found in textbooks and brief journal articles.

The list of eminent contributors to this series assures the reader expert treatment of the areas covered. The monographs are designed for consumers with varying familiarity to the counseling and guidance field. The editors believe that the series will be useful to experienced practitioners as well as beginning students. While these groups may use the monographs with somewhat different goals in mind, both will benefit from the treatment given to content areas.

The content areas treated have been selected because of specific criteria. Among them are timeliness, practicality, and persistency of the issues involved. Above all, the editors have attempted to select topics which are of major substantive concern to counseling and guidance personnel.

Shelley C. Stone

Bruce Shertzer

URBAN POOR

STUDENTS

AND GUIDANCE

JULIUS MENACKER

UNIVERSITY OF ILLINOIS AT CHICAGO CIRCLE

HOUGHTON MIFFLIN COMPANY · BOSTON

NEW YORK · ATLANTA · GENEVA, ILL. · DALLAS · PALO ALTO

Library of Congress Catalog Card
Number: 75–141288

ISBN: 0–395–12047–0

TO
MAURICE AND ANNA MENACKER,
WHO RAISED THREE URBAN POOR CHILDREN
WITH MUCH LOVE AND ATTENTION

v

CONTENTS

EDITORS' INTRODUCTION

For many years it has been traditional and convenient to blame the plight of the poor either upon individual shiftlessness or, at the other extreme, upon all the weaknesses and ills of society. Neither alternative is useful today, for the factors which are bound up with poverty are now recognized as varied and intricate. Such factors as the complexity of urbanized life, widespread affluence that illuminates poverty all the more starkly, too long a delay in providing equal educational opportunities, and negative expectations held by and for the poor can be cited, to mention but a few.

Students whose economic background are substandard are of special concern to the schools. It is recognized that unequal educational opportunity has often produced handicaps in reading, as well as other basic skill subjects such as English and mathematics. An attitudinal disability which is equally pervasive, destructive to future advancement and difficult to overcome is the self-defeating view held by many impoverished students. This attitude is endemic to the outlook of many urban poor students.

Certainly, high priority should be given to establishing programs designed to meet the challenge of educating people from economically poor homes. What is perhaps of prime importance is that young people who might otherwise become disillusioned in their quest to be useful and productive members of society be infused with a personal sense of worth and dignity.

Julius Menacker, the author of this monograph, sets forth some of the salient characteristics of urban poor students, and describes and illustrates some specific guidance strategies which are basic to communicating and working with urban poor students and are essential to changing their environment. In addition, he advances some notions related to the preparation and role of the counselor who would serve such youth. We believe that the reader will find that Menacker's work reflects the honesty that originates from insight gained through much experience with those about whom he writes.

SHELLEY C. STONE
BRUCE SHERTZER

AUTHOR'S INTRODUCTION

Poor people have always comprised a significant proportion of the population of American cities. In earlier generations, the school was viewed by these people as a most important means of gaining the preparation needed to move up the social and economic ladder. The efforts of the schools combined with the burgeoning economic opportunity and manpower needs of American society generally provided good opportunities for advancement. Today, a contracting labor market for the unskilled and the impatience and awareness fostered by the civil rights movement have resulted in more questioning of the intentions and procedures of the school than ever before on the part of poor people. Educators themselves have recognized the inadequacies of schools to prepare urban poor students for full participation in current American society.

Inner-city schools are starting to change and innovate as they attempt to serve the present generation of urban poor students. A critical aspect of school service in this regard is the guidance function. Through properly executed guidance, students can be helped to adjust better to the demands of school and the school can be helped to serve clients better. Also, guidance personnel should contribute to improved dialogue between parents and other adults in the community served by the school and the professional educators employed in the school. In order to accomplish these objectives, guidance personnel must develop new attitudes towards their work with the urban poor, new techniques of accomplishing their objectives and more concern for the long-range effects of their work. Effective guidance for urban poor students demands that counselors reassess their past and present roles and ferret out that which has not proven successful regardless of how beneficial particular practices may have proven with middle-class students. Bold new guidance approaches must be developed and implemented if the schools of the cities are to cope with the very real educational needs of urban poor students.

JULIUS MENACKER

Urban Poor Students
and Guidance

Clarence Williams attended a high school located in a black ghetto near the center of the city of Chicago. His teachers were continually sending him to his counselor, who served as disciplinarian, attendance officer, vocational and college consultant, test administrator and interpreter, and personal counselor to over 700 students. The counselor's main relationship to Clarence was as a disciplinarian. Clarence was not disruptive or antagonistic in class, and he had a reasonably good record of attendance and punctuality. He upset his teachers because "he just sat there." His apathy, indeed his profound indifference to the business of the class was manifested by napping during the period or simply staring into space, completely oblivious to the events taking place around him. His teachers were better at coping with overt discipline problems than with his stolid, unremitting apathy.

The harried counselor was near the end of his patience and about to expel Clarence from school when the chance intervention of another student produced the information from Clarence that his usual diet consisted of a breakfast of "sorghum" (a type of molasses) and bread, no lunch because he lacked the funds, and an evening meal invariably dominated by starches and carbohydrates. It seemed reasonable to assume that this sub-standard diet could have been the main cause of Clarence's poor classroom performance. The school nurse, who spent two days a week at this school of 5,000 students, confirmed the probability that there was a strong relationship between Clarence's diet and his poor academic performance. Operating on this assumption, the counselor secured a job for Clarence in the school lunchroom, which provided him with a well-balanced lunch. The school nurse arranged for a medical examination which established the fact that he was suffering from malnutrition. Since Clarence's family (his mother and five siblings) was supported by public welfare funds, the family social worker was contacted, which resulted in assistance to the mother in planning more nutritional meals. After several weeks, Clarence ceased being a problem to his teachers and began performing at an academic level that, while not exemplary, at least allowed for him to pass his courses. He eventually graduated from high school, and it seems safe to assume that had it not been for the intervention of the counselor and others solicited by the counselor, he would not have done so, due in large measure to his undernourished condition.

Truman Hatfield was a seventeen-year-old boy who had twice been expelled from this same high school. His second expulsion had been punctuated by a near physical attack on his counselor that was narrowly averted by the timely appearance of the school policeman. Truman was a boy with unusual theatrical ability. The high point of the school year for him always had been the annual talent show, in which he had, at one time or another, participated as master of ceremonies, singer, dancer, and actor. After this November show, his attendance, behavior, and academic performance would always plummet to the point where school custom dictated his dismissal.

Truman was given a third chance at completing high school in the fall following his second dismissal, because two new factors convinced his counselor that this time there was a better likelihood of success. In the interval between his second dismissal and the beginning of the next school year, the school had instituted a drama course, and it was taught by an intense, devoted teacher who was also a professional actor. The counselor had discussed Truman with the new drama teacher, who agreed to take special interest and time with him. The new semester saw the drama teacher making Truman his special concern, both in school and outside of the school. He managed to involve Truman in outside theatrical activities that included a part-time job as a stage hand, and he served as Truman's tutor, not only in drama and English, the field of his B.A. degree, but also in other subjects where he was able to be of help. He convinced Truman that there was an important relationship between verbal skills and knowledge in general to success in the theatre, and that he had the natural talent that could lead to a successful theatrical career. The result was that Truman graduated from high school at the age of twenty, and went on to study acting, on scholarship, at the drama school of the Art Institute of Chicago.

These true cases represent exceptions to the usual results of guidance in schools serving urban poor populations, where most often, students like Clarence and Truman leave school permanently to seek unskilled, low-paying employment that serves to further confirm the view formed by their school experience, that American society has little to offer them. These cases are presented in order to illustrate the two major strategies that guidance specialists may employ with urban poor students to improve the academic adjustment and performance of their clients. The first case was an example of a counselor intervening to help manipulate the student's environment in order to facilitate his ability to cope with the demands of school. The second illustration shows the guidance specialist helping the student modify his behavior to improve his school performance through improved motivation and aspiration. The former case involved intervention in the home conditions and physical sustenance of the student, while the latter case involved altering behavior by introducing opportunities for the student to realize deeply held aspirations.

These two guidance strategies for urban poor students — intervening to assist in manipulation of the student's environment and helping the student to cope with the school program through behavioral alterations (Weinberg, 1968) — constitute the major foci of this monograph. Either approach presupposes a model of the counselor as an activist — a doer and intervener — a catalytic agent willing and able to move people, change conditions, take chances — mainly, someone who is willing to *do* things. So much of present-day school counseling theory is geared to the counselor as one who "counsels"; i.e., someone who sits and talks to students about problems and suggests solutions or attempts to have the student discover the source of his problem and develop his own solution, that the term seems somewhat inappropriate to this model. Also, the typical school "counselor" in a ghetto school is immersed in a variety of other guidance functions and related clerical activities that makes for a very confused role regardless of the objectives set for the individual. Therefore, the term "guidance specialist" will be used along with "counselor" to accent the ambiguity that exists in practice and highlight the necessary distinctions that should be drawn in school guidance functions. In discussing the drawbacks of traditional concepts of counseling when dealing with the disadvantaged, Gordon (1967) makes the same point by writing that we must "discourage the practice of guidance as primarily a symbolic, vicarious experience in the exploration of self in relation to a hypothetical or synthetic world."

It should be recognized that traditional guidance practices, which emphasize assisting the student in self-direction through presentation of the results of assessment instruments and information about occupational and educational opportunities, supplemented by verbal interactions between counselor and student have been generally accepted as meaningful and appropriate for American schools. One important reason for this is that the social and educational assumptions that permeate the philosophy and goals of the guidance program and the school are in harmony with the values, aspirations, abilities, and backgrounds of the majority of the population served by the schools — the middle class. These traditional practices do not suffice for the children of the urban poor, who are not equipped by material conditions, prior experience, or psychological disposition to take advantage of them. Gross (1969) contends that many of the most basic assumptions made by the counselor about his relationship with the disadvantaged student are incorrect. The assumptions that he calls into question are as follows: (1) the client comes voluntarily; (2) the client wants help; (3) the client accepts the authority of the counselor; (4) the client comes as an individual and is so treated; and (5) the counselor accepts the client. He contends that approaches which capitalize on group affiliations, self-help, and self-identity would be more effective than current attempts at client-centered therapy.

The inappropriateness of traditional guidance practices for urban poor students is symptomatic of the larger problem, which is that the city schools do not provide the students with adequate educational opportunities and experiences. Efforts are being made to correct this situation. Pilot programs such as New York's Higher Horizons Program have demonstrated, according to Hechinger (1967), "what really needs no proof — that a heavy investment of money and talent in superior instruction leads to a high rate of educational success." It has also been held that similar investments in additional guidance services can be expected to produce demonstrably beneficial results, such as reductions in dropout rates (Tannenbaum, 1967). Current reviews, however, indicate that these early claims of success for programs offering intensive services have not been nearly as valid as initial evaluations suggested. Even if this simplistic solution was indisputably true, we must realize that we cannot expect massive inputs of money and personnel to be generally forthcoming for all areas of need in the inner-city, at least not in the foreseeable future. Nor should we become particularly dependent on this approach, not only because its efficacy has been called into question, but also because it holds the insidious danger of overpowering the student and forcing him into school-made molds that may distort more natural routes of beneficial intellectual and social growth. Instead, the guidance specialist should objectively evaluate the wisdom of being party to concerted efforts to fit the student to the long-range objectives of the school. In many instances, it will become clear that the more appropriate strategy is for the counselor to work toward adjustments in the school in order to meet the short-range needs and desires of the disadvantaged student. The counselor can assist in this by mediating between the school and the student in order to motivate the school to adapt to particular student needs. Owens and Steinhoff (1969) make this point in ascribing the failure of New York's More Effective Schools program to the schools' unresponsive organizational climate, which persisted despite massive inputs of new money, personnel, and programs.

One exemplary effort currently attempting to meet the educational needs of urban poor children through a change in teacher-student climate is the Independent Learning Center of the Ray Elementary School of Chicago (Wiley, 1969). The purpose of the Learning Center is to provide individualized instruction on a part-time or temporary basis to students released from their regular classes. Generally, the children sent to the Learning Center have learning difficulties, but students who could profit by a more enriched program than is possible in the classroom also participate in the center. In one case, a child's poor academic performance was diagnosed as an inability to maintain extended concentration on school work. When sent to the Learning Center, the student was allowed to explore the stock of games and toys; work with the small computer, read books, or engage in conversation with the professional staff that was available to him. He eventually became interested in the Monopoly game and, with the help of the staff, became quite proficient at the game. While playing, he exhibited more sustained concentration than he had ever shown before. Some of this new ability to concentrate was transferred to his classroom work, and definite improvement in his school work was soon evident.

The boy still has a long way to go in achieving a normal level of school performance. The important thing is that the first step forward has been taken. The student had been met on his own terms and his most immediate and basic educational need was diagnosed and treated without large doses of verbal interaction, but with definite changes in the atmosphere in which staff and students interacted. Guidance specialists could profit by the example. No structured counseling was employed, but there was appraisal of the student's needs, and behavioral change was promoted by altering the school environment for the student.

There would be no need for a "Learning Center" if our ghetto schools accomplished the announced task of all American public schools, i.e., to meet the needs of their students. By the same token, guidance specialists would have no need to do anything "special" in treating the urban poor if these children were in an educational environment that met their individual needs (Gordon, 1969).

It would be most difficult for the counselor to be successful in either helping students change their behavior or altering their environment if interaction was confined solely to the guidance specialist and the student. At various times, it may be necessary to involve teachers, principals, peers of the student, parents, social workers, community leaders, psychologists and many others. The ability to utilize these persons in assisting the student in making behavioral and environmental adaptations is of critical importance. This ability is as important as the need for good personal interaction and rapport that must exist between counselor and client. The guidance specialist's strategy should be to develop a "total interaction process" (Daniel, 1967) in which human and material resources are marshalled by the counselor in support of the educational needs of the student. The crucial person in the process would still be the counselor, or to be clearer in terms of role definition, the guidance specialist. He would continue to use counseling as a basic tool, but there would be other tools that would also be utilized — people, money, the help of other institutions, food, medicine, and all the other human and material resources available in such great abundance in this country, however unequally they may be allocated. Every inner-city community is set in a larger community containing vast industrial and commercial enterprises and huge pools of human expertise. The guidance specialist must be able to employ techniques that utilize these resources to the student's advantage. One example of an unconventional use of community resources would be for the counselor to solicit funds from the industrial-commercial community for establishing scholarships to be awarded to needy high school students so that they would have the funds necessary for them to cope with school. Some funds might be distributed on the basis of need and merit; other funds might be disbursed solely on the basis of need. Both methods are currently employed, through funds provided by the national and state governments, for the assistance of college students. Since similar needs exist on the high school, and even elementary school level, guidance specialists should see beyond the traditional usages of the concept of student financial aid and see to it that the concept becomes a reality for poor students at any educational level. Governmental reluctance to break traditional practice should be combatted, but since the needs of poor students are immediate, private sources should be pursued.

The guidance specialist, then, is more than a counselor; he is, to use a military analogy, logistics, quartermaster, planning, operations, and infantry support for the student. Success at this task requires that the guidance specialist win the support and confidence not only of students, but also teachers, administrators, parents, community leaders and members of the other constellations of people that may be utilized, from time to time in support of a student.

The problem of role definition is not restricted solely to the counselor of disadvantaged children, who most often comes from a middle-class background and has been trained along traditional lines that emphasize verbal interactions or "counseling sessions" as a central theme. The students whom they are to serve are equally confused about the role the counselor is to play in relation to them. These students view counseling services as a rather fragmented aspect of the total school program, not without some significant negative connotations (Grande, 1968). Similar feelings are often held by inner-city teachers, themselves the products of the same middle-class milieu as the guidance workers, as well as school administrators and parents. The success of the counselor will, in large measure, be dependent on his ability to clearly define his role, not only for himself, but for the students he intends to assist and the other people, within both the school and the community, who can play significant roles in altering the student's environment or his behavior.

Guidance workers must come to grips with the proposition that it well may be that the low achievement of students in slum schools is primarily due to the low expectations about their learning capacities held by teachers, and a general unwillingness or inability on the part of the school administration to make the necessary adaptations of curriculum and school organization needed to provide learning conditions that better meet the particular needs of these students (Niemeyer, 1968). The work of Rosenthal and Jacobsen (1968) provides striking evidence of how teacher expectations of inferior performance on the part of poor students, lead to inferior performance by their students. They contributed much insight into the power of teachers to effect self-fulfilling prophecies through their experiment which provided slum teachers with false test scores indicating high intelligence levels for particular students. The result was that higher teacher expectations resulted in higher student performance. In such situations, the guidance specialist may find himself to be in the key position within the organizational communication network to act as an effective change agent to produce more sensitive teacher attitudes as well as changes in curriculum and general organizational climate.

There can be little argument about the importance of parental attitudes toward schooling for their children as an influence on success in school. In the inner-city, as anywhere else, there will be parents who support the school, those who oppose it, and those who are ambivalent and apathetic about it. A major failing of guidance in slum schools is that it has not been successful in marshalling parental support for the school program, and generally has failed even to establish an adequate system of meaningful communication between the school and parents. The counselor must realize that it is not enough just to offer his good offices to these parents and wait for the offer to be accepted, as it might with middle-class parents. Many of these parents do not know how best to help their children to succeed in school, and many also lack the expertise in formal organizational participation to become involved with the school in a meaningful way (Schindler-Rainman, 1967). Even so, school personnel are gaining a new awareness and respect for the positive potential that these people have for improving ghetto education. Earlier coalitions of parents and other interested ghetto citizens into "concerned parents" groups that brought important school changes to serve student needs better, used disruptive, aggressive techniques. We are now seeing the transition to more sophisticated methods of promoting changes, as the poor become more adept at working with the schools, and as the schools, ever so hesitatingly, open their councils to parents. The guidance specialist should be involved in the confrontation and dialogues between the community and the school to help channel these relationships into the effective and harmonious patterns of school-community relations so vital to the total educational environment of the child.

The one unalterable condition that the guidance specialist working with urban poor students must face is the need for change. Initially, this may mean changes in the attitudes and techniques of the guidance worker himself, and in faculty and administration. Changes in the school program is another factor. The guidance specialist must also act as both a promoter of needed changes in these areas and as an instrument assisting in changes in the student's behavior and his out-of-school environment. Those involved in producing such changes can sympathize with Hoffer (1952), when he wrote:

> No one really likes the new. We are afraid of it. It is not only as Dostoyevsky put it that 'taking a new step, uttering a new word is what people fear most.' Even in slight things the experience of the new is rarely without some stirring of foreboding. . . . It needs inordinate self-confidence to face drastic change without inner trembling.

The guidance specialist does not have total responsibility for effecting meaningful change in the school, community, and the behavior of students. The administration has the most direct and pervasive responsibility, and teachers, community leaders, parents and students themselves also play roles as change agents. Counselors can best function as change agents by either working directly with the student to introduce behavioral changes needed to successfully cope with school, or by actively involving himself in assisting the student to establish a more beneficial environment for education. Either role will require the counselor first to gain the trust and confidence of the student. Another requirement will be expending the necessary time and energy for an adequate assessment of the student and the forces that impinge on his education. This involves inquiries about the student's health, academic ability, financial resources, home environment, peer relations, aspirations, relationships with teachers, his views about the role of the school as it affects him, and whatever else might be an influence on his present condition and future development as a student.

When these pre-conditions have been met, the guidance specialist will be in a position to begin to interact meaningfully with the student and the other persons in the particular aspect of his environment or behavior on which attention has been focused. The counselor must go to these persons with a plan for improvement that clearly delineates the contributions these persons, or the student himself, can make toward improving his educational situation. Finally, the counselor must have the willingness and ability to marshall these people and whatever available resources (money, clothing, food, books, housing, et al.) have been identified, into action that will resolve problems in the most concrete manner possible.

The task set for the guidance specialist working with the urban poor, then, is to promote meaningful educational change through both psychological guidance, which involves working directly with the student and others in producing needed behavioral changes, and the sociological approach, in which resolution of the educational problem requires utilizing people and resources both inside and outside of the school to restructure the physical or social setting that impinges upon the student's educational progress. The procedure involves establishing rapport with the student through student assessment, developing a corrective plan, contacting the necessary persons and resources needed, and finally, utilizing them in a manner which produces the desired results. The considerations involved in doing these things represent the subject of this monograph.

2

The Characteristics of
Urban Poor Students

William Hilton had shown promise from the time he entered elementary school. He always got high grades and performed at or above grade level on standardized achievement and intelligence tests. He stayed true to form in high school, graduating in the upper five percent of his class, with good college aptitude scores. Also, he was commander of his high school R.O.T.C. unit and a member of the all-Chicago R.O.T.C. honorary squad. His college experience was no different, as he earned the B.A. and M.A. degrees in American literature. At the time of this writing, he is twenty-six years old and earns an above average income as Coordinator of Special Programs at the University of Illinois, Medical Center Campus. He has already published an article in a national professional journal and serves on several state and national committees on college admissions and related matters.

The unusual aspect of this true story is that Bill Hilton is black and came to Chicago at age seven from South Carolina with his illiterate mother and father and two sisters. He was raised in the North Lawndale area, which has the highest rates of crime and poverty in the city. The rate of dropout and "throwout" of students from high school exceeds fifty percent. Bill's father never earned more than a marginal income, working variously as a "ragpicker," janitor, or handyman. Although Bill's story could be duplicated by examples from every large city in America, his academic and professional success is unique for the products of this nation's urban ghettos and is hard to explain, given the deprivations under which he grew up.

The example of William Hilton serves to underscore an axiom that should be kept in mind whenever generalizations are made to characterize large, disparate groups of people: *There are more differences within any group of human beings than between groups.* There are Puerto Rican and Appalachian white youngsters living in poor urban areas who would succeed in any society, regardless of the obstacles, just as there are others in the same community who would probably not be successful even with all the advantages bestowed upon the most affluent elements of our society. The same is true of white suburban students and all the other various categories of children in the United States.

Generalizations must be made, however, in order to understand the important phenomena taking place in contemporary society. Urban poor students are mostly Negro, but also include significant numbers of Puerto Rican and Mexican youngsters, whites who recently migrated from the impoverished hill country of the South and border states, and smaller numbers of American Indians and first and second generation children of Europeans who by choice or circumstance have remained outside the mainstream of American culture. It is difficult to generalize about such a diverse collection of peoples. Yet, certain characteristics that have particular relevance for education can be generally applied to all of these groups. First, the schools have been unsuccessful with them because of the environmental, physical, and psychological deficits which they bring to the school and because the schools have not been sensitive to their needs. They live in the most crowded and dilapidated areas of the cores of large cities and move about frequently from one sub-standard residence to another. They have a high incidence of learning disabilities and below average achievement levels. The well-known labels of "culturally deprived" and "socially disadvantaged" are apt descriptions from the perspective of middle-class society. If there is a bias in the generalization of characteristics found herein, it is toward the Negro group, which constitutes the largest single sub-group in urban poor populations.

The children of the poor and under-educated have less opportunity to achieve academically and to find social and economic success. This is due to environmental conditions that include economic deprivation, physical and mental health deficiencies, differences in home and school language, home and family problems, peer group relations and norms that may not support school practices and norms, unavailability of appropriate role models, and the counter-productive attitudes of important social service agents such as teachers, social workers, and policemen. Overriding all of these environmental factors is the importance of the generalized lack of faith these children and their parents have in the ability of the educational system to benefit them, and the parallel feeling of personal inadequacy in coping with the demands of the formal system of education. These two elements are so strongly related that it becomes difficult to separate them for any but theoretical purposes. All of these factors contribute negative elements that militate against the ability of the public schools to properly serve these children when traditional concepts of education are utilized.

The City, Home, and Family

The city has always attracted the poor because it offered them opportunity. However, the chance for economic and social benefit afforded by the diversity of enterprise and society in the city has not been without its costs. There has been a severe loss of status and sense of belonging to a larger society compared to the stable, if oppressive, relationships of rural and less advanced societies. The inhospitableness of their new urban life spurred people to group together according to race, religion, old world antecedents, or similar standards. The continued poverty of many of these individuals and groups dictated that these in-gatherings would take place in the least desirable sections of the city. Where these groupings did not occur voluntarily, they were often forced by the dominant majority. Groups entering the cities during earlier times found conditions that allowed them to break the bonds of voluntary and imposed ghettoization and rise to membership in the middle class. Most of these people were Europeans. It is ironic that the most recent wave of urban immigrants, who are primarily American citizens, have not found it as easy to move up the socioeconomic ladder as had the foreigners who preceded them. The main reason for this is, of course, deep-seated racial prejudices held by the majority of Americans that are much more intense than the national and religious prejudices that made advancement difficult for many earlier immigrant groups. This prejudice has produced a lifestyle for many of these new urban immigrants that includes poverty, welfare dependency, unstable families, and dead-end, unskilled jobs. All this comes with the child when he enters the schools of the city.

Many of these children come to school with far greater exposure to basic human problems and privations, and the emotions and acts that follow, than most middle-class teachers would experience in a lifetime. In this regard, the students are "older" than their teachers, creating a problem of role relationships between them. Life in city slums acquaints the child very early with the existence and effects of narcotics, prostitution, organized gambling, alcoholism, and the total range of crimes of violence motivated by passion or profit. In such an environment, one must learn to cope with physical dangers that render life in an urban ghetto a hazardous existence. Shootings and stabbings are not uncommon among teenagers, and gang membership is often a necessity for a boy not willing to abide almost daily intimidation, extortion, and beating. Children are often left to fend for themselves on the street for long periods of time, and they learn to survive the hazards of traffic, bullies, perverts, and disease with a courage and skill that makes growing up to be reasonably adjusted adults an accomplishment in itself.

Money is always a problem with families living in urban ghettos. The most obvious effect of poverty for many children is seen in the poor clothing they wear to school. A more intimate knowledge would reveal a lack of "pocket money" and funds for such ordinary expenses as lunches and minor school supplies. A less easily discernible factor that militates against coping with school is that dire poverty forces some parents to view their children as economic liabilities that must be converted into assets. These children are encouraged to find employment, at an early age, and many of them need no such encouragement, for their poverty is as real to them as it is to their parents. They may start by delivering groceries or shining shoes, and by about the mid-teens, the pressure for substantial earnings forces many of them, particularly boys, to drop out of school and take whatever full-time jobs they can find. Others are dropped from school for truancy or poor performance caused by night jobs that sap their energies and ambition. Many of these youngsters are glad to leave school because even the tentative prospect of a full-time salary is much more appealing than the vague, delayed financial rewards promised by the school for those who stay and graduate. Too many of them have seen high school graduates unemployed or holding jobs no better than those held by early-school leavers.*

An investigator wishing to isolate the conditions in Bill Hilton's youth that helped him rise above the obstacles of his environment might point to his good fortune in having both a mother and father

---

* A 1969 report of the Detroit Volunteer Placement Corps revealed that only five percent of the graduates of inner-city high schools were placed in jobs, college or job training programs by fall, while fifty percent of the dropouts scheduled to be graduated with the same class had found employment (*Newsfront,* 1969).

in his home from earliest childhood to adulthood. There are so many instances among the urban poor where this is not the case, that this factor does seem to be an appropriate distinction. The result of this circumstance and the frequent inability of the father to provide adequately for the family, is a matriarchal home, which works particularly to the disadvantage of the boys, who have no adult role model in the home and who have been betrayed by their sex.

Home life is complicated by living in overcrowded, sub-standard apartments, where there is much sound but little communication. The focal point of life at home is typically the television set. Children compete with the television set for each other's attention and, among themselves, for the parents' attention. The adults are burdened with problems of simple survival and coping with an environment that continually reinforces feelings of inadequacy and hopelessness. The result can often be a pattern of rigid child-parent relationships, where physical punishment predominates in a pattern of immediate and spontaneous rewards and punishments (Daniel & Keith, 1967). There is little dialogue between parent and child, and desatellization from parents in favor of the peer group occurs at an early age. Advice is sought from siblings and peers more often than from parents about education and related matters, but these peers are no better equipped with answers than the parents, and lack at least the maturity and more extensive experience possessed by the parents. Even in those homes where communication among parents and children is abundant and harmonious, it contributes little to preparing children for the demands of school. This is so because of the sub-cultural "in-group" style of verbalization which is quite different from the vocabulary and style of verbalization that will be encountered in the school.

It is often assumed that these parents are not concerned about the education of their children because they do not interact and relate to school personnel in accordance with the expectations of these persons. In some cases this is surely true, but more often this attitude reflects the belief that the school does not represent a realistic route to advancement for their children. For other poor city people, this lack of support for the schools results from subsuming the school into the complex of public services and agencies they have learned to stay away from. The public assistance office, the police station, parole and probation departments all represent authority and problems rather than assistance. The school, as another public agency close to their lives, shares in this negative connotation (Schindler-Rainman, 1967).

Most of the representatives of these agencies appear to be primarily concerned with checking on people to make sure that they have not violated an agency regulation or that they are not taking unfair advantage of the public largess. There are few positive elements in such relationships. The social worker checks to see that earnings have not exceeded established standards for maximum assistance benefits and that the husband and father has not re-entered the home. Some policemen act to prevent trouble before it happens by heavy-handed intrusion on people, particularly boys, in complete violation of the civil rights of the individual. They have little time or concern for problems brought to them by ghetto residents, and the residents soon learn to realize this. The same behavior styles are practiced by other social service representatives in the ghetto, most of whom come from environments alien to the one in which they work. It is, therefore, no surprise that the poor learn to respond to these people by evasive, noncommittal behavior. The ghetto resident sees the relationship not as a helping one, but rather as one requiring them to match wits with the social service person to see that a minimum of harm results for them, and that they extract as much benefit as possible from these sources to which they must often turn for simple survival.

The behavior styles practiced by inner-city schools have not done much to dissuade people from this view. Parents are called to school or contacted through phone or mail primarily to be presented with problems relating to the truancy, discipline or academic failure of their children. The presentation of these problems is often accompanied by threats of school expulsion or transfer to "special" schools for the youngster, or threats of court actions or reductions in public assistance payments for the parents. The parents' response to this is similar to that made to the parole officer or social worker, which emphasizes antagonism and hostility at worst and apathy at best. An example of how poor people translate this attitude into practice when dealing with public agencies is the characteristic sometimes referred to as "minority standard time" (Schindler-Rainman, 1967). This is the tendency of poor people to have little regard for punctuality due to their experiences with endless waits in clinics, police stations, and similar places. They have learned that a 2:00 p.m. clinic appointment usually means waiting two hours to receive fifteen minutes of the doctor's time, so they tend to arrive late. This lack of punctuality is usually taken to be a sign of indifference or hostility by the school counselor. It may not be that at all. It may simply be a matter of abiding by established custom when dealing with public agencies. Clearly, an unproductive relationship generally exists between parents and the inner-city school. For a number of reasons, the school has been considered enemy territory by the poor, and the school has done little to change that impression (Mauch, 1969). Many parents who view the school favorably and wish to cooperate are handicapped by not knowing the proper approaches for connecting with the school, and the school typically does not have the expertise or willingness to involve these parents in a meaningful way. Research indicates that participation of urban poor adults in educational affairs and activities strengthens their interest in education and their view of its importance (Cloward, 1963). The evidence now becoming available from recent experiments in community control of schools, as in New York's Ocean Hill-Brownsville and Milwaukee's District 201, tends to confirm this judgment.

The appearance of indifference in the encounters of poor parents and school counselors belies the evidence accumulated to support the very strong and urgent aspirations they hold for their children. It is true that these aspirations may often be unrealistic when viewed against the cold realities of the student's abilities and resources. The discrepancy between the effort and sacrifice needed to even begin working for these goals, and the willingness of poor parents to make these efforts and sacrifices is often very great indeed. To the guidance professional, these aspirations seem to be almost expressions of fantasy unrelated to real events (Katz, 1968). It is a rare circumstance when these aspirations are accompanied by meaningful long-range plans for accomplishing these high-level educational and occupational goals (Vontress, 1968).

The relative inability of low-income parents to cope with their environment is communicated to the child along with a generalized attitude of passivity, defeatism, and intermittent hostility, which often has the effect of a self-fulfilling prophecy that condemns the child to repeat the failures of his parents. This indicates a severe need of urban poor students for appropriate role models. A study of 52,000 low-income dropouts in New York City indicated a failure to perceive a meaningful relationship between the activities of the school and their future expectations. Also, the respondents indicated that they had few relationships with adults who had the ability to help them in either goal clarification or goal attainment (Gottlieb, 1967).

The Peer Group and Role Models

Early independence from parents makes the role of the peer group and adult role models outside the family extremely important determiners of the urban poor student's accommodation to formal education. Despite the fears of many lower-class mothers, the peer group assumes much of the socializing role normally handled by the family in American society. The peer group becomes the child's main source of values and the group from which he derives his status (Amos & Grambs, 1968). Particularly for boys (but not exclusively), the peer society means gang society. Juvenile gangs in the inner-city recruit like eighteenth-century British naval press gangs. Those refusing to join are liable to periodic beatings and other forms of intimidation. Many determined students avoid gang membership, but the physical and sociological costs can be high. At the very least, it is necessary for the boy to find a strong peer sociogroup outside the gang complex with which he can identity. A loose family structure in which parents and relatives are seen to be defeated, unfulfilled people, intensifies the need for strong peer group membership and identification.

Identification, according to Bruner (1966), refers to:

> the strong human tendency to model one's self and one's aspirations upon some other person. When we feel we have succeeded in being like an identification figure, we derive pleasure from the achievement and, conversely, we suffer when we have let him down . . . We extend our loyalties from an individual to a reference group . . .

The isolated social space afforded to the disadvantaged makes the search for identification with typical American success models extremely difficult. More often than not, the only available identification figures are those in the neighborhood, and they are comprised totally of poor minority group members or the officials of social agencies such as teachers and policemen. This has the effect of turning the youngster more deeply inward to peer group members, who share common educational and socio-economic disabilities. It is of critical importance that this insularity be broken down so that the inhabitants of urban ghettos may have a wider range of role models from which to choose and find reinforcement. There is evidence that disadvantaged youngsters who view lower-class occupations and life negatively can and do identify with middle-class adults (Henderson, 1967).

In the classroom, poor students are inhibited by their peers from operating at top performance levels. The typical underprivileged boy fears that achieving academically will cast him as feminine (Vontress, 1968), while the girls that excel get little recognition and encouragement for it, since the concept of a "career girl" is not part of low-income culture. As with most school-age peer relationships, individuals are reluctant to appear different from their fellows or violate group norms. In the case of the poor, one of these norms is disinterest and resistance to the school program which, one would suspect, has a causal relationship to the traditional inadequacy of the school for them. These norms also include values that reward the flouting of established authority, postures of toughness, and apathy in the school setting. Even the means they employ to gain acceptance, identification, or recognition within the classroom (aggression and defiance) conform to a group norm that is counter to the standards of behavior imposed by school authorities (Duncan & Gozda, 1967). This all combines to handicap the disadvantaged youngster in the setting of formal school education.

The Urban Poor Student As A Learner

The first prerequisite for any child, if he is to perform in school at anywhere near his capacity, is physical well-being. The poor, of course, are the most likely group to suffer ill-health. Serious disorders are recognized late and treated in public health facilities which are overcrowded and overworked. It is a rare lower-class child who has the benefit of periodic medical checkups, or even professional treatment for all but the most serious disorders. Many go through long periods of time suffering under the debilitating effects of undiagnosed illnesses. Some slum schools have minimal medical services, but the medical professionals must fight not only a problem greater than the resources available to cope with it, but also a communal behavior pattern that inhibits many students and their parents from freely revealing the condition of the child's health. This is but another dimension of the syndrome of mistrust and hesitancy these people have when dealing with governmental representatives in any form. One study (Welter, 1968) that is instructive in this regard indicated that the most striking result of a summer experiment that brought counselors and their ghetto clients together in a camp atmosphere resulted in the discovery of many more health and health-related problems than even the most experienced counselors had thought existed. It is certainly true that many deprived youngsters are performing below expectation and become behavior problems and truants due to ill health. These disabilities may range from slightly impaired sight or hearing to tuberculosis. Whatever the particular infirmity, it is likely to nullify the effects of the teacher and the school in proportion to the seriousness of the health impairment (Bloom, Davis, & Hess, 1965). The fact that ill health is prevalent enough to be considered a "characteristic" of the urban poor is indeed a sad commentary on the sense of social responsibility in our society.

Another elementary learning handicap shared by most typical slum-bred children is a language orientation that places an immediate, persistent gulf between them and their teachers. The home and neighborhood have conditioned them to interact in a different style of verbalization than is customary in school settings. The paucity of "classroom" language found in family interaction is transferred to the peer society both in and out of school. Boys find reinforcement for adding to this a pattern of limited verbal interaction in line with their sub-cultural view of talk as feminine, as opposed to action, which is masculine. They prefer physical acting styles of expression to verbal communication. Probably the most fluent, varied and creative use of language is seen in its use as an instrument of aggression (J. E. Gordon, 1968). Those who have seen slum children in arguments or engaged in good-natured kidding of one another would be shocked by the same youngster's verbal limitations when engaged in conversation with a school counselor. They feel this handicap of inability to express and interpret their feelings through the use of conventional verbal symbols, and it becomes not only a verbal handicap to communication, but also a psychological impediment to free interaction with the counselor (Gordon, 1967). The language of lower-class children in school tends to be restricted in form, and it serves mainly to communicate signals and directions rather than complex thought processes or elaborate points of view. This is in counter-distinction to the elaborated school language of the upper and middle classes, which serves to communicate ideas, relationships, feelings and subjective states (Bernstein, 1961). Counselors and other school personnel are, of course, more representative of the upper and middle classes than the lower class.

The result is that guidance specialists and teachers have a hard time in understanding the attitudes, problems, and aspirations of the disadvantaged, and these youth, in turn, find it equally difficult to make their inner-selves known to school professionals. The disadvantaged student also does not have the ability to find learning cues in the verbal and written language forms used by the school staff. Many of them simply have not assimilated the modes of reception and expression that are traditional prerequisites for academic success (Gordon, 1967). These children possess two languages: a restricted middle-class "school" language used in the classroom and similar situations and a second language which, as in the case of Latin-Americans, is a formalized language that they can use for a far greater range of expression. In the case of black youngsters a sub-cultural language exists that allows for communication with peers along much more subtle and meaningful lines than is permitted by use of their "school" language.

Urban poor students are not as motivated by aspirations of academic and vocational achievement as their middle-class peers. The degree and direction of school-related motivation for them is often inconsistent with both the demands and goals of formal education. It is important, however, for guidance personnel to understand that although the quality of aspirations may be depressed, it is usually consistent with the student's perception of the opportunities and rewards available to him (Gordon, 1967). According to Hyman (1953), these youngsters have less optimism about the possibilities for advancement, less belief that personal effort is an important factor in who gets advanced, and less belief in the rewards of work. The role models available to them in their slum environment provide daily reenforcement of that view. They become aware of "the subtle cultural cues which tell you that you don't count and that good grades and high I.Q. scores are middle-class roads to success, not yours" (Loretan & Umans, 1966).

The will to learn is an intrinsic motive that finds both its source and its rewards in its own exercise (Bruner, 1966). It can be thwarted in the school through rigidly imposed curricula, regulations, reward systems, and patterns of human relationships. The deleterious effects of these things upon the urban poor are more serious and severe than for other groups of students. Any student, even the most advantaged, has an adjustment problem in school, with its increased requirements for restraint, orderliness, neatness, and verbal rather than action oriented modes of response and interaction. It is exactly in these qualities that the poor are most deficient. The school should respond by altering conditions so that the positive attributes of these children are emphasized and developed in reaching educational goals (Reissman, 1962). Unfortunately, this is not often the case. Not only does this cause many students to have difficulty in coping with the demands of school, but some simply stop attempting to cope with the problem, and instead adopt a behavior pattern designed to defend against entry into the problem. These are two different sets of problems with different sources of motivation. Bruner (1966) explains this distinction by using the analogy of the person playing tennis who has the problem of trying to win, as opposed to the person who expends all of his energy simply trying to stay off the tennis court. Both of these conditions prevail among urban poor students. The former case presents a problem in helping the student to learn; the latter requires interesting the student in trying to learn. The effective guidance specialist must understand and be able to assess these distinctions and other learning problems if he is to adequately assist the disadvantaged.

Poor children are best motivated by rewards that are both immediate and concrete. They have difficulty in seeing the relevance of school since they are unable to fully comprehend or accept the deferred and symbolic gratification system that the middle-class student has come to accept as a matter of course (Bloom et al., 1965). There is a strong relationship for them between motivation and immediacy. They have learned from their parents and other deprived adults, as well as from their own experience, that the future is uncertain, and that there is little value in planning ahead. Put another way, these people have not had reinforcement in the pattern of long-range planning and effort to achieve desired goals. They see no logical pattern to their lives — things just happen (Loretan & Umans, 1966). Poor people accept the pattern of following momentary urges and taking what is available immediately, for tomorrow one may not be able to do or get it, or indeed, one may not even be around at all tomorrow (Schindler-Rainman, 1967). They live with a sense of impermanence, of transiency, of all things being temporary.

This orientation to immediate and tangible gratification on the part of the poor has implications for guidance as well as learning. Terrel and others (1959) found that middle-class children learn more quickly when given a non-material incentive than when given a material incentive. The reverse was found to be true for lower-class children, who tended to learn more quickly with material incentives. This finding supports the opinion that the psychological set of disadvantaged youth demands "something more earthy and material than the lure of self-improvement or some distant goal" (Amos & Grambs, 1968). The disadvantaged operate in the present, on the basis of a short-run hedonism. Unfortunately for these children, the American school system is structured to complement the deferred gratification and non-material incentive patterns of the more advantaged segments of American society.

As important as these characteristics are for understanding and meeting the educational needs of the urban poor, they pale in importance when compared to the matter of the student's attitude toward himself. The most serious educational deficiency of the disadvantaged student is his feeling of inadequacy when confronted with the expectations and assumptions of the middle-class school. The student soon begins to devalue himself and accept the notion that accomplishment as defined by the school is impossible for him. This leads many to attempt to establish some positive self-identity by rebellion against the school. More often, the experience leads to apathy, which becomes a far greater problem for inner-city educators than unruliness (Schwab, 1968). The student's lack of orderly work habits, his low interest in the purposes and content of education, and a life style far less socially inhibited and much less structured toward the achievement of deferred goals, combine to produce early and repeated failure, which erodes one's pride and saps the courage necessary to attempt more and more complex tasks, which is, of course, the premise of the school curriculum.

A study of school dropouts (Niemeyer, 1968) reports that most of them have known mostly failure in school. The causes of failure were laid not only to the students' inability to master basic academic skills, but also to the school's inability to give them, among other non-academic needs, a sense of self-respect. The self-concept of failure takes root, and often before the end of elementary school, it becomes a self-fulfilling prophecy. The negative self-image of the disadvantaged within the social system of the school and the psychological milieu of middle-class American life propels them further into the social fabric of slum society. They meet the basic psychological need for self-esteem by rejecting the values of the school and the society it represents. Instead, they bestow acceptance and esteem on those who similarly have failed to cope with the educational system. Some leave the school, feeling as one would upon being released from prison, because for them the school has been little better than a prison. Others leave convinced that they are failures, and carry this psychological scar for the rest of their lives.

3

Considerations and Methodology for Guidance of Urban Poor Students

Regardless of the professional orientation that the counselor brings to his assignment, there are particular methods that he will find most efficient in working with urban poor students. The special problems and needs of urban poor students require that traditional techniques and tools of guidance be adapted to forms that are more appropriate to the inner-city. Some might need to be discontinued within urban poor schools, regardless of the strength of tradition. It may also prove useful to develop completely new approaches that fill voids in guidance services for urban poor students that had not previously been attended to. Finally, it is of critical importance that even the most basic presumptions of guidance work be reevaluated to insure that the efforts expended do serve the interests of the disadvantaged.

Communicating With Urban Poor Students

The prime requisite for assisting students to cope with school is the ability to communicate with them in a meaningful way. This requires that the counselor be sensitive to the emotional subjective overtones his speech and communication style have for his charges, and it also imposes responsibility on the guidance specialist to learn the language styles of the disadvantaged so that he can understand the student and respond in ways that are fully comprehensible. The speech of the urban poor is sub-cultural. This is to say that many words, gestures, inflections, and other communication signals they use do not correspond to middle-class rules, although the vocabulary is English.

The counselor must take the position that his responsibility is to communicate with the urban poor, not improve their language usage. This means that just as the disadvantaged student must learn to be facile with standard English to meet the requirements of the class-room, the counselor must learn and develop fluency in the communication style of the lower class if he is to be effective (Orem, 1968). Part of that style involves less dependence on verbal fluency and more use of gestures and tonal statements. The words used by a boy who is the product of an urban ghetto may often appear disrespectful to a middle-class counselor. It is important for the counselor to understand that this may be the natural mode of expression for him and, indeed, the use of natural speech patterns may imply more respect and confidence for the counselor and the existence of better rapport between the two of them than if the student felt constrained to use "classroom English" within the confines of the counseling relationship. A black inner-city high school student may be given to calling the counselor by his first name, simply as a confirmation of the equality that is supposed to exist between them. He might say that he must drop out of school because he needs a "slave" to earn "bread" to "keep up his crib." The functional guidance specialist would accept the first name reference and understand that the student was telling him that the need for a full-time job to earn sufficient funds to pay for his housing is forcing him to drop out of school. The counselor should not attempt to affect the student's language style. Attempts of middle-class counselors to use sub-cultural language usually come across as artificial and as de-meaning to both the counselor and the student. Some words or ex-pressions that come naturally are fine, but there should not be a conscious effort to imitate the student's speech patterns. It is not neces-sary or desirable. Disadvantaged students can understand conventional English.

As many of the urban poor become increasingly militant, this be-comes reflected in their communication style. The tendency of some to call the counselor by his first name is one reflection of this militancy. Again, if the counselor concentrates on the task of communication, rather than concerning himself with traditional decorum, he will ac-cept this condition and concentrate on improving communication. As the counselor involves himself in dialogue with urban poor students, he should be alert to pick up the meaning of sub-cultural communication which, while more restrictive than the dominant communication pattern, contains a great amount of subtlety and versatility.

In order to listen to and understand the client, the counselor must insure that they can talk in a quiet place, without fear of interruption. It is a good idea to set a time limit for the meeting and, even if this must necessarily be short, it is preferable to a long counseling session that is interspersed with interruptions. The student may relate much that is not fully understood in all of its implications. If so, it is much better for the guidance specialist to indicate that, than to pretend to grasp all the subtleties the student is trying to convey. The lack of total comprehension will make itself evident anyway, as the counselor begins to respond, so it would be much better to proceed from the outset in a frank way. In his responses, the guidance specialist should resist the temptation to philosophize and draw general analogies to the student's problems, particularly those related to the counselor's school experiences, for this will most often be unreal and meaningless to the client. The student, after all, generally comes from quite a different background than the counselor, with all sorts of important differences in the way the two would view particular events and their relationship to present and future conditions. It would be best for the counselor to confine himself to providing pertinent information and clear-cut advice that will lead to the solution of immediate problems. For this communication to be successful, it is necessary that an atmosphere be established in which the client feels free to tell the counselor when he is perceived to be on the wrong track and offering unacceptable or unworkable solutions.

Even before the dialogue can start, of course, the student and the counselor must be brought together. Many traditional assumptions and procedures underlying school counseling must be eschewed in producing contact between the guidance specialist and his disadvantaged client. Amos and Grambs, in the introduction to their book (1968) have highlighted this problem very well by stating:

> We are now beginning to realize that the very forces which make so many young people of the slum and depressed areas unemployed and unemployable also keep them from seeking help — that this is *part of the problem*, not a reason for evading it. . . . Going out to reach the youth on his own grounds, may be essential to success in later counseling.

The guidance specialist must take the initiative in contacting the student. He cannot simply sit in his office and wait for students needing assistance to seek him out, for some will, but most will not. The guidance specialist must get out of his office to visit with students during their lunch periods, at sporting events, away from school at community events, and the many other points of contact that are available. The counselor must be armed with information about the students he wishes to contact and must be prepared to offer them help and be bold enough to make contacts on grounds that are, either physically or psychologically, the student's "turf" rather than his own. It would be a mistake for a counselor to contact a student without some definite ideas about the deficiencies they are laboring under, and some available resources and a clear plan for help. This plan should be revealed to the student in terms of short-term solutions to problems that the student agrees are present for him. It should be quite some time before long-range or abstract concepts are introduced.

As the counselor establishes a relationship with the urban poor boy or girl, he should keep in mind that these students do not need sympathy, nor do they want it. Indeed, they are more likely to reject it, even while maneuvering to obtain concessions from the counselor based on the commiseration evidenced by the counselor for the student's plight (Schwab, 1968). The relationship may involve an extensive testing of limits in which the student shifts from aggression to compliance, from clarity to obscurantism, constantly trying to manipulate the counselor to serve his own ends. It often seems as if the deprived student were trying to define the counselor as the source of anticipated failure or rejection, or even trying to bring about that rejection so as to preserve the defenses and adaptations he has developed from invasion of such emotionally risky feelings as hope (J. E. Gordon, 1968). Another approach is for the student to attempt to adopt the guidance specialist as a friend, in order to place him at a disadvantage when the student asks for concessions and special favors that would not normally be allowed. The answer to these and similar strategies and attitudes on the part of the student is for the counselor to set clearly defined boundaries prescribing the limits of action appropriate to the counselor-client relationship, and certain standards of interaction. Only in this way will it be possible to establish a line of communication between counselor and client that could be conducive to positive results.

Altering Negative Self-Concepts

The fact that a student rebels in school or leaves school permanently does not necessarily mean that he carries a negative self-concept because of this. It may be that the school has really been little better than a prison for the student, and he leaves it because he correctly senses that it has no relevance or value for him. It may also be that the student leaves school because he feels it is necessary if he is to preserve his inner sense of dignity, which he finds under continual attack in his educational setting. Finally, leaving school might simply represent a realistic choice of alternatives, in which he sees better immediate and long-range potential in a job that is presently available, than would be afforded by waiting to complete school. Still, there will be many students who carry concepts of themselves that severely restrict their ability to succeed in school. The counselor should be sensitive to this and work to correct harmful self-concepts. This negative image can take two forms: An inner-directed self-defeatism which is sometimes close to self-hatred, and an outer-directed, negative self-concept manifested by aggression and antagonism to school personnel and others who are not part of the urban poor community, and are blamed for the self-perceived deficiencies of the student. Both are equally destructive to the individual, but require different treatment strategies.

The Defeatist Self-Image

There is an ancient Hebrew proverb which asks the question: "If I am not for myself, who will be?" The implied answer to this question is "nobody." The pattern of interaction between urban poor students and their counselors has borne out the wisdom of the proverb. Counselors burdened with excessive student loads generally spend little time on students who do not demand immediate attention. The counselor's day is taken up with the serious discipline case, explaining to a parent why her son was dismissed from school, obtaining the verification from a clinic doctor needed to take a pregnant girl off the enrollment record, checking out a report that a student has a gun in his locker, and similar matters that militate against all but the most energetic guidance worker's scheduling time for "average" students or for dealing with less critical but equally important educational matters. This leads to a tacit agreement between the counselor and his clients that they should stay out of each other's way. In many cases, this attitude serves to confirm for the student the accuracy of his defeatist state of mind. This confirmation by the school receives reinforcement from the home and the neighborhood, and in this way becomes pervasive and overwhelming. This helps produce a high incidence of failure and early school leaving, followed by a life of unrewarding, tenuous employment and human relationships.

The clearest remedy to this psychological defeatism is found in providing the student with the opportunity to develop pride in himself. There is no substitute for pride in oneself, and this cannot be instilled vicariously. It can only come from the student setting goals that are meaningful and difficult to him and then, through his own efforts, accomplishing these goals. The counselor's role in this should be to assist the student in goal clarification and understanding the problems involved in accomplishing the goal and the best means of overcoming obstacles to the goal. The guidance specialist can also provide concrete help to the student, as long as this does not interfere with the clear recognition on the part of the student and others who may be concerned, that the establishment and accomplishment of the goal was the result of the student's efforts.

The Hostile Self-Image

There are many students who have learned to view their poverty and the instability of their personal lives as the result of an ubiquitous, unrelenting oppression directed at them from society at large, which includes the school. These are the students who struggle for pride, but are forced to find it outside the reward system of the school and middle-class values. Since they find the avenues for pride and success offered by the school to be unattainable, they hate the school and the people who maintain it. Their need for pride, then, takes other forms of expression. Many of these forms are self-destructive but some, in recent years, have been quite constructive. One example of this is seen in the black youngsters who have adopted "Afro" hair styles, which are both an expression of pride in their race and heritage and a rejection of certain degrading forms of imitation of Caucasian concepts of decorum and beauty. If the civil rights movement had resulted in nothing more than the adoption of such individualistic expressions of self-pride among black children, all the costs and turmoil that have been part of the movement would have been worth it on that count alone.

Unfortunately, there is a negative side to this new militancy, which propels the student into rejection and hostility of the school and the values associated with it. This may not necessarily mean that these students reject education per se, but rather they may simply be opposed to some of the expectations and procedures used in their school which is dominated by middle-class values. The guidance specialist must, first of all, accept such students on their own terms, and enter into dialogue with them. There must be a climate in which the student can freely express himself, within limits that prevent personal abuse to the counselor or behavior that is so disruptive that it obviates the possibility of any constructive results.

When two-way communication has been established, the guidance specialist should expose the student to realistic alternatives to his militant psycho-social orientation, and provide him with the opportunity to test these alternatives.

More often, it will probably be better to encourage the student in his militancy and efforts at achieving distinctiveness and a sense of identification with a prouder, more inspiring social mystique than they had previously known. The counselor should turn this aggressiveness and hostility into more acceptable and beneficial channels than is the case at the start of the guidance relationship. This may mean encouraging the student to protest poor laboratory facilities or outdated textbooks, as a substitute to his ubiquitous hostility to the school and staff generally. The object is to transform generalized hostility into hostility against specifics that deserve hostility, and channel aggression into paths where it can be seen as demonstrably beneficial to the student's education and an effort directed towards achieving acceptable educational conditions. The guidance specialist must tread carefully in this role, for it would be easy for the student to misunderstand this support as being an attitude condoning attacks on the school for their own sake, which it should not be. Teachers and administrators must be made aware of this tactic for the good of the student, and so that the counselor can preserve his effectiveness in relating to his colleagues. The end result of this approach could easily be that the student gains better understanding of the school and his role in it, as destructive emotions become channeled into constructive avenues. Again, it is important that the choices be made by the student, and that whatever success is achieved be due to his own efforts. Even so, there are helping roles that the counselor can play, while avoiding patronizing the student or doing his work for him. One can be fairly well assured that evidence of a desire to help but not interfere on the part of the counselor will be returned, at some point, by the student's respect and support.

Appraisal of Urban Poor Students

All too often, pat feelings of "knowing" the deprived child are based on acquaintance with the abundance of literature dealing with these young people. This information can contribute a good deal to improved understanding and assessment, but it can also cause guidance personnel to deal too much in generalities for assessing their students. Counselors must remember that they are in the business of appraising *individuals* who may all be disadvantaged in one way or another, but who do not necessarily fit into the same molds for purposes of treatment (Barclay, 1967). Often, middle and upper class students suffer by comparison in some generalizations of urban poor children. Here is an impression (Schwab, 1968) presented by a middle-class teacher upon starting work at an inner-city school:

> In a city high school of 3,000 Negro students . . . I found more musical and dramatic talent than I had seen in a state university of 25,000 in the whole four years I attended. The talent shows resembled Birdland in comparison with the pantomimes and silly dance routines that I remember as being the substance of such shows in my own suburban high school.

It is no more true that black students have more theatrical talent than suburban white students, than it is that white students are more capable of learning than black students. Too much generalization in either direction is dangerous and destructive to the guidance specialist who is in the business of assessing and helping individuals. This requires that he employ a framework for assessment that subsumes great variation of individual traits under categories of appraisal most appropriate to what we know to be common characteristics of urban poor children and the treatments they receive from counselors and other school personnel.

Physical Assessment

When confronted with a situation requiring student assessment in a general way, the counselor should proceed in accordance with the laws of parsimony, which dictate that basic physical needs be determined and dealt with as a first step (Walz, 1969). Children who may seem lazy, apathetic, or dull in school may be suffering from malnutrition. Others may have deficiencies in sight or hearing. The incidence of tuberculosis among poor city children is very high, as are cases of high blood pressure and many other easily hidden but seriously debilitating diseases. These physical problems may go undetected for years, as harrassed teachers in overcrowded classrooms ignore symptoms of illness and counselors concentrate on psychological and emotional adjustment. Referrals should be made to the school doctor or nurse, if one is available, when there is any indication at all that the student's academic problems may have a physical basis. If no medical staff is available, contact should be made with the nearest community public health agency. The physical education teacher is generally the best resource person on the academic staff to check with about suspected health problems. Community persons and social workers are also sources from which corroboration or information about health problems may be obtained, in addition to the obvious techniques of discussion with parents and the student himself. It is, of course, imperative

that the parent be kept well informed throughout the process of identification, referral and treatment of physical problems.

Many new counselors tend to discount as fabricated excuses the
stories of illness told to them by students attempting to justify sleep-
ing in class, extended absences, leaving class abruptly, and similar
acts. This should not be the attitude of the guidance specialist because
of the precarious health environment of the urban poor. It would be
time well spent if every story told by a student in justifying tardiness,
absence and the like was checked out. Many times, the result of this
will be the discovery of diseases that can be arrested with proper treatment or, in any case, should be treated. Eradication of some of these
afflictions can lead to dramatic reversals in school performance, while
in other cases, identification may mean the difference between life and
death.

The Use of Tests in Appraisal

Testing serves a multitude of important purposes in the operation
of a school program, whether the school is serving a wealthy or a
poor population. Among these purposes are assessment of student
readiness for particular learning experiences, school promotion, determining needs for special service and other attention for particular
individuals, class grouping, and course placement. It is not only true
that "when a school superintendent feels that tests discriminate against
the culturally underprivileged child and orders their removal . . . he
surreptitiously opens another door to other tests, as he must" (Bernstein, 1967), but it is also true that there have been no "culture-free"
tests that have convincingly demonstrated their utility as assessment
instruments that can duplicate the many purposes that tests now serve
in school guidance (Wechsler, 1967). Further, while it may be true
that many commonly used standardized tests and even some "home-
made" tests are biased in favor of middle-class culture, it is equally
true that our school programs and requirements are also biased, in that
they primarily reflect the dominant culture and attitudes of American
society. Given these assumptions, it behooves guidance personnel to
select tests wisely, to interpret test results in relation to the circumstances of the testees as well as in relation to test norms, and to use
test results not as confirmations of hopelessness for urban poor students, but as instruments to diagnose student needs. Just as a gun can
be put to both good and bad uses, so can tests in the hands of
counselors.

The use of intelligence tests in appraisal of urban poor students
can serve as an example of the utilization of testing instruments to
the advantage of these students. David Wechsler (1968) states that:

It is true that the results of intelligence tests, and of others, too, are unfair to the disadvantaged, deprived and various minority groups, but it is not the I.Q. that has made them so. The culprits are poor housing, broken homes, and a lack of basic opportunities.

The test results should serve to identify to school personnel the educational needs of the student. They should not serve as the impetus to a categorical label for the student, and will not, for those who accept the possibility of the continuing plasticity of intellectual development of poor students (Gordon, 1967). Because of the deprivations experienced by most of the urban poor, it seems most appropriate for Bernstein (1967) to write that "the culturally deprived Negro child who scores at I.Q. 85 is not stupid. His I.Q. is equivalent to the I.Q. 100 of a middle-class white child." He believes that removal of some of the barriers to intellectual development can and have produced remarkable results. Intelligence is a mixture of both heredity and environment and can be changed by redirection of goals and values, and by hard work. Regardless of genetic structure, man is adaptable, trainable, educable, conditionable, and alterable.

Poor test results merely serve as evidence that the socioeconomic conditions of the disadvantaged have not allowed them to achieve their potential. Test scores can and do fluctuate as a result of changing educational conditions. Dramatic increases in the standardized test scores of students in such enrichment programs as Higher Horizons and the Great Cities Project provide evidence of this (Daniel, 1967).

One important obligation of the guidance specialist is to interpret tests results for teachers. In far too many cases, the worst by-product of the inner-city school's testing program is the subtle influence of the test results on teacher attitudes toward their students. Many teachers, consciously or unconsciously, expect the level of performance from the student that is indicated by his test scores, as was so vividly indicated in *Pygmalion in the Classroom*. The counselor must work with the teacher to make her aware that the slum child is handicapped in taking tests by low motivation, fear of unfamiliar formal situations, and a general lack of competitiveness in the intellectual realm. These factors not only lower the validity of the test results, but may also make the results unreliable from one testing situation to another. Interpretation of results is further complicated by the tendency of these students to cluster at the bottom of the normative distribution, which obscures the differentiations among individuals within the school group (Fishman, 1967). The counselor should emphasize to administrators and teachers that these factors demand that test results, particularly intelligence tests, be used as very broad, general indicators of student ability that can be considered only one measure among several in making decisions about student capabilities. The firmest assumptions should be made for those students whose scores place them well above or below their peers. Teachers must be convinced that the results cannot be considered as a static point from which the individual can never move. The educational obstructions that are imposed on the disadvantaged and the fluctuations in educational conditions that are usually part of his school career, suggest that beneficial conditions could produce rapid rates of improvement in intelligence scores, reading levels, and other areas measured by standardized tests. This is true not only at the elementary school level, but it is equally true at the high school and even the college level. The introduction of an intensive program of guidance and academic assistance for disadvantaged students admitted to the University of Illinois at Chicago Circle produced dramatic leaps in achievement on standardized tests for those students who were admitted with substandard test scores. Many of these students moved up four and five grade levels after only ten weeks at the University. The counselor should help the teacher develop the attitude that the remarkable thing about the test scores of so many disadvantaged students is not how far below average they are, but rather that the students have been able to achieve as well as they have, considering the obstacles under which their education has been conducted.

Test results of disadvantaged students should be used for purposes of diagnosis. The task of the educator is to ponder what lies behind the test scores. One might properly address himself to the question of how a student managed to achieve an I.Q. score as high as 90, or a grade level reading score while suffering under deprived socioeconomic and intellectual conditions. Another valuable approach to diagnosis is attention to the *rate* of improvement on standardized tests rather than simply the achievement level. Periodic spurts upward, or even more important, consistently bigger performance gains, indicate the promise of a great reservoir of untapped potential to be unleashed by proper guidance and teaching. Standardized test results also provide guidance specialists with the opportunity to diagnose reactions and responses to specific test items which offer clues to the needs for particular experiences or remedial work.

New standardized testing instruments need to be developed that are better at appraising the intellectual levels and needs of disadvantaged students. Since very little progress has been made in that direction, guidance specialists must make the best possible use of those instruments presently available to them. They may find it helpful to supplement standardized tests with "home-made" tests that better reflect the backgrounds of their charges.

Other Appraisal Techniques

The pattern of guidance in many urban school systems has been four or five hours of testing for every hour of counseling (Daniel, 1967). The reverse of this pattern would seem to be more in line with the needs of disadvantaged children. Since standardized test results and other data from group studies do not lend themselves to adequate assessment of the disadvantaged (Cody, 1968), other techniques of assessment must be used in conjunction with test results. Interviews with students, parents, teachers and others who know the student or have an influence on his education should be employed. Present limitations in this direction are indicated by a study revealing that in New York City, the average number of counselor interviews with each student is about one a semester (Tannenbaum, 1967). The ratios in other school systems with large numbers of disadvantaged is similar. This is caused not only by inordinately heavy counseling loads, which may run well over 600 students per counselor, but also by the responsibilities of testing, record-keeping (much of it designed to gather evidence to justify student dismissals), and similar tasks that are tangential to the guidance function. These conditions severely limit the ability of the counselor to appraise his charges properly. Further limitations stem from incomplete, inaccurate, or even missing cumulative record files for students who have moved about, to and from many different schools. The high transiency rate of inner-city teachers and counselors also hampers the good record-keeping necessary for proper appraisal, which must involve a *total* assessment of the student.

The sad state of appraisal resources should stimulate innovation. One tool that might prove useful in the absence of more detailed information about the student's past history would be utilizing a school para-professional as a student research worker. It would be the task of this person, preferably someone raised and living in the community served by the school, to develop histories on students requested by the counselor. This would take the researcher into the community to talk to peers and adults who had known the students, visits to schools the student had attended to talk to the student's former teachers or consult old records, perhaps visits to hospitals and clinics that might have records on the subject, and whatever other sources of information seem to present themselves.

The counselor could utilize teachers in securing current information about the student that would be pertinent to the guidance relationship. For example, the teacher might be asked to develop a sociogram of the class in which the subject is located, if this kind of information is both needed and justifiable as part of the classroom instructional program. English teachers could be asked to make autobiographies written by particular students available to the counselor, with the concurrence of the student. Many other "gerry-rigged" assessment techniques can be developed. These are certainly not adequate substitutes for a well-organized, professional assessment program. However, until adequate resources are provided, these improvisations will prove better than nothing. In 1965, the Chicago Board of Education recommended a ratio of counselor to client in disadvantaged high schools of one to two hundred (Crow, Murray & Smythe, 1966). That recommendation has yet to be put into practice.

The Counselor as a Role Model

Given the great variety of personality differences that exist among any group of human beings, it is difficult to generalize on what type of guidance specialist can have the best effect on any particular student. For example, a black student from the ghetto might be best served by a black counselor because the student would feel more comfortable with him and be able to relate to him easier. Later in his school career, this same student might receive the best help from a white counselor. Sex and age, as well as race, may be factors determining the ability of the student to relate to or accept a particular guidance specialist as a role model. Although the needs of the student should be taken into account in developing a counseling relationship, it is generally true that the most important factors in building rapport and identification are the concern and the competence of the guidance specialist. When these qualities are exhibited, the guidance specialist will be more likely to gain the student's confidence and respect, even if he is of a different race and sex, than another counselor who matches the student's race and sex but does not exhibit these professional qualities to the same extent. One of the several beneficial end products that may occur when a counselor has reached this relationship with a client is that he can serve as a role model for the student. This can fill a desperately important, yet unmet need for the urban poor student. This does not mean the student will aspire to becoming a school counselor to emulate his model, but rather that the student will identify with elements of character and behavior exhibited by him.

Differences of race and social class between counselor and client are not nearly as critical deterrents to identification as is commonly supposed. There is abundant evidence to suggest that lower-class children are able to and often do identify with middle-class persons, and that if a lower-class black youngster feels it is bad to be lower-class, then lower-class adults of any race will be rejected as role models or advisors by him. Also, the theory that only blacks can counsel and teach blacks ignores the many middle-class blacks who reject lower-class blacks and vice-versa (Henderson, 1967).

J. E. Gordon (1968) suggests that counselors are in a good position to serve as role models for disadvantaged students who are: 1) lacking in self-esteem; 2) have difficulty in meeting task requirements; 3) are dependent; and 4) have a history of failure. There are certainly enough urban poor youth who meet the requirements of those criteria. Another element that should be added to Gordon's criteria is the student's need to obtain a clear role definition for himself. It is this condition, more than the others, that renders the client susceptible to the influence of the counselor as a role model. The guidance specialist who would serve as a role model must be willing and able to extend his relationship with the student beyond those activities related only to school adjustment. Most important, the counselor must be willing to give of himself, in terms of time and emotional energy, to enhance the relationship. This involves giving information about personal background, aspirations, problems, and other data that will allow the student to gain the personal insight needed to form the strong bonds of identification that can lead to adopting the counselor as a role model.

The value of providing role models for the poor student stems from the paucity of adequate adult models in the student's out-of-school environment. Suffice it to say that without adequate role models, whether they be found at home, in the community or at school, the psycho-social development of these youngsters will be less favorable than would otherwise be the case. An adequate role model will allow for the kind of identification that gives a student self-direction and a view of himself that motivates him to work for success in school and accept the deferred gratification and non-material incentives that had been followed by the model in his days as a student. Another reason for the importance of finding role models for urban poor students is that they will serve to compensate for the tendency of these students to over-identify with a peer group model that has standards of behavior and achievement which do not contribute to academic and vocational preparation. Even when adequate role models do exist, the strong pull of peer group identification cannot be ignored as a powerful motivating force in the student's development.

Group Guidance and Counseling

The importance of peer group influences on urban poor children has led J. E. Gordon (1968) to attack individual counseling for these students as inadequate, because it is inconsistent with their group loyalties, which usually take precedence over all other human affiliations for them. He believes that the resistance of these youngsters to the individualizing pressure of one-to-one counseling causes them to enter psychologically into this relationship only as a delegate of the group. One result of this attitude is that the student withholds any personal commitment while engaged in individual counseling. Fagen (1968), in arguing against too much individualized counseling for the disadvantaged, suggests dyadic and triadic rubrics for counseling as a more preferable option. He feels that they are more in harmony with and better reflect the importance of group membership to these youngsters. He faults guidance specialists for treating the disadvantaged student as an "anti-collective" in spite of the compelling evidence of the strong collective spirit of these children.

The position of Fagan and J. E. Gordon is too extreme in that they advocate the total discontinuance of individual counseling for the disadvantaged in light of the strong influence of the peer group. A better approach would be a balanced program that included some individualized counseling but emphasized group guidance. The predisposition of urban poor students is to be natural and spontaneous in group situations, as opposed to their reticence and uncomfortableness in one-to-one counseling situations (Walz, 1969). Therefore, group guidance should be used to develop communication and solicit information from slum children. The skillful guidance specialist can lead the discussion from initial hesitancy or flippancy on the part of students to discussions of mutual concern for them, often in areas that they would hesitate to openly discuss individually or even collectively in their own informal environmental setting. Group counseling for the disadvantaged is also effective in helping them to objectify and discharge emotional conflicts (Blodgett & Green, 1966), particularly as these conflicts relate to problems students have in common in adjusting home and community values with school values.

In this group setting, the guidance counselor is allowed a freer, more dynamic role than he usually can have in counseling urban poor students individually. The atmosphere that allows students to lose many of their inhibitions and constraints also allows counselors to interact on a lower tension level, where they can express views and raise issues that would be either offensive or hostile to many of these students if initiated in an individual setting. Further, the counselor has the opportunity to discover in casual, indirect ways, much more about the motivations, aspirations, fears, and problems of his clients than would usually be possible in individual sessions. Again, the reasons for this are the natural and spontaneous behavioral tendencies of the disadvantaged in group situations as opposed to individual sessions with counselors, and the fact that having one counselor relating to several students "evens the odds" in the minds of the students, allowing them to relax and be themselves, while gaining frequent reinforcement from their peers as dialogue expands among the participants.

Vocational Guidance

The outlook of the urban poor about vocational opportunities is severely restricted. Many of them have never been much beyond the confines of their neighborhood, perhaps three or four miles square. The older people around them have had minimal or sub-standard educations and hold the kinds of jobs that typically fall to people so ill-prepared. They are laborers, unskilled factory hands, domestics, and service workers in restaurants and hotels. They are, as the well-known expression goes, the last ones hired and the first ones fired. Long job tenure is rare and occupational advancement even rarer. This is the occupational perspective that the children of the urban poor bring with them to school.

These young people, then, have not had the opportunity to learn about and develop aspirations for vocations that come as a matter of course to middle-class children, who have informal interaction with adults in many rewarding vocational fields. Frequently, poor students do not even have the reading and library skills to develop good vocational aspirations through the abundant vocational literature found in the guidance departments of many schools. This makes it more difficult for counselors to assess latent or budding vocational objectives through traditional aptitude tests, interest inventories, and discussions. Since the student does not have the background to take advantage of the broad range of vocations implied in these techniques, discussions of vocational choice between the counselor and his urban poor client become limited by the restricted range of direct and concrete experiences related to vocations that is in the possession of the student (Amos & Grambs, 1968). This is not an adequate basis for proper vocational guidance and, consequently, much more effort and ingenuity must be expended in the vocational guidance of the poor than is needed for middle-class students.

One recommendation (Bloom, et al., 1965) calls for regularly scheduled vocational guidance interviews to begin as soon as the poor youngster starts high school. The responsible guidance specialist should be thoroughly versed in current occupational information, and combine job placement function with vocational guidance. The vocational guidance specialist must be careful that his own biases about vocational choice are kept out of the relationship with students. Presentation of occupational information to the poor must be done in ways that are more vivid and interesting than the usual booklets and talks. A multi-media approach is desirable, in which television, radio, film strips and motion pictures, books and pamphlets, talks by resource persons, and phonograph and tape recordings are utilized. These should be supplemented by such techniques as career conferences, buzz sessions, a human resources directory, field trips, psycho- and socio-drama, etc. (Feingold, 1968). It is essential that some of these devices be adapted to provide parental involvement, for their interest and encouragement can be a critical factor in producing successful outcomes from vocational guidance. This can be done by scheduling vocational guidance sessions at times that allow parents to participate. This participation should include not only voicing opinions, going on field trips, hearing speakers, and the like; but it should also involve parents in decision-making roles about the vocational topics to be covered and the manner of implementation.

The most valuable resource for vocational guidance is the city itself. Every urban area contains living examples of the scope and variety of vocations available in America today. The city can be transformed into a vocational guidance classroom without walls, which would not only be excellent vocational guidance but also broaden the social and cultural awareness of the students. The cooperation of business and professional people would not be difficult to secure for having students as guests in training sessions for new employees conducted in many large industries, or to have a few students observe the practice in a professional office. The possibilities are almost limitless. It merely requires guidance persons to make the necessary contacts and arrangements.

It is important that the educational requirements of various occupations be stressed. Career presentations might be organized in categories of educational requirements. There would be presentations on careers requiring high school graduation only, then those needing a two-year college degree, a bachelor's degree and so on. The experiences that supplement verbal and written presentations by the counselor should include both the educational and occupational facets. For example, the presentation of pamphlets about the data processing program at a local junior college by the counselor would also include a short explanation of the preparation involved and the characteristics of occupational life in that field, as the knowledge of the vocational guidance specialist would allow. That should be followed by a visit from a student or teacher, or both, who are involved in the program. Then the students should hear from someone who has graduated from the program and is working in the field. Finally, there should be a visit to the college to observe the instructional program and facilities, and then a visit to a typical computer installation that employs graduates of the program. This approach is particularly sound for the urban poor, in light of their need for concrete experiences as motivating forces.

The role of vocational guidance is of critical importance to the academic motivation of urban poor students. Research reveals (Cloward & Jones, 1963) that their evaluations of the importance of education are directly influenced by their occupational aspirations. Therefore, vocational guidance must be an integral process in the total guidance program. The introduction of this facet of the guidance program might well start before Bloom's recommended time of the first year of high school. It would be better to start in the elementary school. The sixth grade would not be too early.

The Involvement of Parents and Other Adults

The objectives of guidance are much more easily accomplished when supported by the students' parents and other persons who have influence with students. It is also true that the effectiveness of a counselor who is supported by these significant others will be much increased (Brookover, 1967). When the counselor presents an evaluation of the student and his potential that conflicts with the evaluations or aspirations of parents or significant others, it is doubtful that the student would accept the evaluation of the guidance specialist. Therefore, it is important that the guidance specialist establish contacts with these adults to develop a system of consistency between the school, home, and community in regard to those attitudes and behavioral patterns that involve guidance concerns.

Adult involvement for guidance purposes cannot be secured in poor communities without guidance personnel taking the initiative by getting out in the community in both day and evening hours. There is no substitute for this elementary and essential ingredient. This may require the counselor to frequent pool halls, taverns, or street-corner gathering places at times. More often, however, it will mean visiting boys clubs, community centers, urban progress centers, the local YMCA or settlement house. The criterion that will determine which place is visited is the location of the adults who have the greatest influence on the students. If the local pool hustler is the idol of some of the guidance specialist's clients, he will be the man to see, rather than the person running the local Neighborhood Youth Corps. These significant others should be allowed to participate in the planning of guidance efforts, particularly those with community implications; just as school counselors should establish for themselves a role of influencing and advising on community programs for their clients.

The guidance staff must be prepared for community persons who are very resistant and unimpressed with them. One of the main reasons for this is that the staff is oriented toward long-range goals that involve delayed gratification for the students. Not only are the typical community representatives more oriented toward programs that offer immediate, concrete results, but they also have little faith that some of the long-range goals proposed by the school can ever be accomplished under present educational conditions. This problem of standing up under day-to-day evaluations and expectations by the community can be met in large measure simply by building an atmosphere in which guidance personnel are perceived as friendly, supportive, involved, and committed to improving the lot of their charges (Gordon, 1969). A good step to take in building such perceptions is extending guidance services to adults into the community. Evening guidance centers to serve dropouts and adults with a variety of educational and occupational concerns would be very effective. A library of occupational information and listings of current job opportunities for adults would be an appropriate service in such a center. Another would be a referral service that could operate both during school hours and in the evenings. The referral concerns would include medical services, family counseling problems, financial assistance, and a variety of other forms of social service assistance that public and private agencies are prepared to render.

The involvement of guidance personnel in the projects and activities of the community is the best way to combat traditional hostility and apathy toward school personnel. This involvement may take the form of soliciting petition signatures for a new stoplight or joining in demands for improved garbage collection, or even participating in activities focused on changing procedures and improving education at the school. This type of commitment will provide the opportunity for guidance personnel to interact with the adults of the community on terms that would promote acceptance and understanding of each other. Also, these activities will provide entrance for school representatives into the newly emerging power structures of poor communities, whose endorsement may soon become a necessary precondition to effective relationships with poor students (Walz, 1969). Just as the barely visible, but highly influential informal power structures of larger social and political units have become recognized as important influences in getting things done or making changes in the community, so too may this soon be the case for those wishing to provide service or promote change in ghetto areas. The well-publicized militant, the formal political leader, shopkeepers, the economic leaders, gang heads and leaders of informal groupings of people will all have to provide consent if the school is to be effective in providing more meaningful guidance for urban poor youth.

Before launching into these community-based activities, the guidance specialist must become aware of an important caveat: the poor do not recognize professional limits for the performance of different guidance services. They may feel that the counselor who can treat a problem of adjusting a student to a particular course at school should also be able to solve a family financial problem, or decide whether or not the child needs a doctor. It is most important for the counselor to clearly delineate his limitations and those areas which are his professional concern. These limitations and concerns must be made clear to the poor family in a way that does not convey the impression of disinterest or shirking of responsibilities.

Relationships with parents are, of course, generally more delicate and intricate than with other adults who are important to the guidance of urban poor children. The counselor must learn about the aspirations that parents have for their children, and respect these views. If, in the opinion of the counselor, these views are destructive to the education of the student, this opinion must be carefully developed with the parents in such a way as to enlist parental support for a new view of the child. It is most important that the parent be given an active role in promoting the fulfillment of aspirations for the student on which the counselor and parent eventually agree. An example of the kind of active involvement that could be developed is a communication system whereby the parent is informed of the homework assignments of the student and in return informs the school about the time the student has for this work. Between the two, arrangements would be made to see to it that the two elements of time and homework are harmonized in the best interest of the student.

It is extremely important that contact with parents not be initiated only as a response to some shortcoming of the student. At that point it is often too late to do much good. Communication with the parent should be introduced as a regular part of the school guidance program as soon as a student is enrolled. This communication should be as natural as setting up a record file for the student, or calling him in for an initial interview. It should be two-way communication in every sense of the term. The counselor should provide information to parents and receive information from them. He should both give advice and be ready to solicit and receive advice from parents. The counselor must be sure to initiate contact and stand ready to receive parents who initiate contact. It follows that meetings with parents should take place not only at the school, but also in the student's home. When the guidance worker feels as much at ease at one place as the other, he has most probably established the rapport and communication needed to utilize the parents in fostering the best possible educational environment for the student.

Parents should be called together from time to time, either as members of a permanent body, as a PTA organization, or on an ad hoc basis to deal with specific problems. The larger-scale continuing organization should be approached along non-traditional lines, in view of its historic failure in ghetto areas. One approach would be to enlist the support of neighborhood clergy, who could organize meetings of school-related groups as part of the church activities. School officials would be invited to attend these meetings, but the fact that they were held at the church, and involved an authority other than just the school, would reduce the alienation and uncomfortableness of parents. Parents would be responsible for the features of organization, rather than being forced to follow the middle-class organizational concepts of the PTA. Instead of regular dues assessments, perhaps they would decide to base financial support on monies received by "passing the plate" as they do at church. It might be that students would be asked to join such a group, too. It is likely that freeing formal parent-school organizations from their traditional mold would make them much more responsive and viable groups for supporting education at inner-city schools.

School initiatives to establish ad hoc parental groups to deal with specific problems will usually be more effective in promoting meaningful involvement. These groups need not be restricted solely to parents, but at times should include other adults in the community, when the nature of the problem indicates that their involvement would be helpful. A case in point occurred at Wendell Phillips High School in Chicago during 1969. This inner-city school had become plagued with unauthorized persons, many of them recent dropouts, coming into the school and creating havoc with classes, lunchroom periods, study halls, and generally creating an atmosphere of disorganization and violence within the school. The school took the initiative in communicating the problem to parents, and eventually formed a group of fathers and other adult males, most of them World War II and Korean War veterans, who donated time to serve as guards during the school day. It did not take them long to end the entrance of unauthorized persons into the school building. It so happened that this ad hoc effort resulted in the formation of a parent, teachers and students group that is to be a permanent school-related organization.

Even without this occurrence, the ad hoc approach had proved effective, and the prospects for other ad hoc groups to convene to solve specific school problems would have been good.

The teachers of the urban poor represent a unique group of significant adults. Not only are they the professional colleagues of the guidance worker, but they are also, in a sense, competitors for professional status in the school hierarchy. While there is a tendency for each group to consider its own role most important, the counselor must realize that part of his responsibility is marshalling resources from as many areas as possible to support student guidance. Therefore, the counselor must take the initiative in promoting cooperative guidance efforts with teachers. This does not mean that the counselor must not disturb or upset the teacher. Indeed, this may often be unavoidable in improving education for the student. In this relationship, however, the guidance specialist must concede that the role of the classroom teacher is central to any effective guidance program (Blocker & Richardson, 1968), for it is the interactions between teacher and student that constitute the fundamental reason for the existence of the school. One of the counselor's concerns is to intervene in those cases where the classroom behavior of the slum child keeps him in constant conflict with his teachers (Butler, 1967). This can be done in a number of ways: by mediating between the two, by working with each separately to increase his understanding of the other, or by removing the student from the conflict situation.

Mediating between the two requires maintaining an extremely delicate balance. The counselor is, after all, a representative of the school establishment, as is the teacher. Both have the same presumed commitment to their students. This could leave the counselor caught between the expectations of the teacher for his support and the expectation of the student that the counselor should better understand him, and therefore defend him. Mediation requires the counselor to acquire sufficient information about the sources of conflict and to represent views fairly to all concerned, which would include the teacher, the students and others who might be indirectly involved. The goal for the counselor is always providing the best learning situation for the student, which may require a change in attitude or behavior by the student, or an adjustment in procedures or expectations on the part of the teacher. Whichever it may be, the counselor must be careful to maintain his autonomy in the situation, so that his partiality is exhibited only to the best educational interests of the student.

In dealing separately with one or the other, the counselor must not make it appear that contact has been cut off with the other party, even when assessment of the problem may require greater interaction with one of the parties. In the extended contact with one or the other, the wider scope of contacts afforded to the counselor should be utilized by him to bring others into the situation. In some cases parents, community persons, or students might help change the attitude of the teacher; in other cases the same types might be used to win over the student to the goals of the teacher.

Every member of the school staff has some kind of guidance responsibility and opportunities for guidance appear in many ways in classrooms and extra-curricular activities (Smallenburg, 1968). The same attitude should be instilled in the student's relatives and other concerned adults from the community. A boys club gymnasium coach who is notified that a student is leaving school early to get more time in on the basketball court, might be much more effective in convincing the student not to cut his last class than anyone else; and he would be in the best position to supply satisfactory alternatives to cutting class. Also, attention to informing community persons with good communication positions about activities in the school and the progress of particular students can result in the extension of the guidance effort into the community in the person of these adults.

The Case Conference

The purpose of the case conference is to provide a formal technique that allows the guidance specialist to call on other useful persons to meet and discuss the educational affairs of a particular student. The case conference has three facets that make it particularly beneficial as a guidance technique in urban poor schools: 1) it provides a setting in which the student's behavior can be viewed from a number of professional and social perspectives; 2) it serves as a training vehicle for teachers by giving them greater insight and sensitivity about students and their problems; and 3) it allows the different professionals to exchange views and better appreciate each other's role. The persons generally included in a case conference, aside from the guidance specialist, would be teachers, administrators, and other school professionals working with the student, as the social worker, psychologist, or nurse. The decision about whom to include should be based on the nature of the problem and an assessment of the contributions particular persons can make to the solution. There may be times when this will mean inviting non-school persons, as parents or community officials, to attend. In general, invitations to parents should be made very sparingly, due to their naturally subjective emotional involvement. The criteria for membership should be representation for all the necessary views of assessment and alternative solutions. Regardless of the problem that precipitated the conference, all participants should be provided with a full medical report on the student, an academic history including test data and a record of class achievement, and other salient features of the student's home and school life.

It should be made clear that any member of the professional staff may initiate the case conference. Also, requests should be accepted from the broader community such as a probation officer, the family social worker or other interested and responsible persons. Teachers or administrators may initiate the conference by directly requesting this of the guidance specialist. More often, the counselor should be sensitive to the need for calling a case conference upon being alerted to a problem student who could be helped by this technique. A counselor might also be motivated to call a case conference to change the attitude of a teacher about a student, or provide administrators with greater insight into student problems.

Each professional member of the conference should be expected to contribute not only by offering insights from his area of expertise, but also in constructing the total resolution or course of action decided upon by the conferees. The counselor would have responsibility for preparing a written report of deliberations and recommendations that would be distributed to the conferees. He would also be responsible for seeing to it that the recommendations are implemented.

The case conference is especially desirable for the urban poor student because it will provide staff members with an opportunity to meet in a dispassionate, unhurried setting to reflect on the needs of not only one individual student, but by extension, all students in the school. It also allows for the teacher to be informed of the many forces outside of the classroom that have influenced the child's behavior. The chief benefit to the guidance specialist is that it gives him a vehicle for marshalling all the diverse persons that can improve the student's situation at one time and place so that a *comprehensive* solution for the student can be devised that considers the *whole* child.

Follow-up and Feedback

The need of urban poor students for immediate and concrete gratification for their efforts requires guidance services to provide prompt feedback to him. When others are involved in guidance problems, whether teachers, parents, or peers, they too should be adequately informed about relevant progress and problems. When the counselor has been involved in initiating changes important to the student's schooling, he must alert the teacher to the need to provide the student with frequent indications of his progress and secure this information for transmission to the appropriate persons outside of the school. The counselor should also maintain involvement in keeping the student apprised of how well his efforts are fulfilling the promise implicit in the guidance he offered the student, encouraging him whenever possible and making him aware of deficiencies that should be corrected.

Feedback should emphasize what Reissman (1962) calls the positive qualities possessed by the disadvantaged student. Build their confidence by using their strengths to overcome the weaknesses they may exhibit when confronted with school requirements that are alien to their backgrounds and aspirations. The counselor who must inform a student that he is reading two years below grade level might view this as a reasonable accomplishment, given the milieu of deprivation in which the student operates. Conveying this attitude to the student does not mean lulling him into a false sense of satisfaction. Rather, it should be stressed that the student must advance faster than he has been, but the student should know that his present level has been no mean accomplishment. Properly presented, this knowledge should encourage the student to increased accomplishment rather than causing him to give up. When the guidance relationship involves creating changes in the school environment or matters that the student has no direct impact upon, feedback to him is equally important.

Feedback can be extended to parents and significantly involved adults in a number of ways. Periodic contacts should be scheduled with parents and appropriate others, regardless of any special problems or developments that may have occurred affecting the student. This regularized exchange will provide a much more balanced picture for adults than would be provided in irregular formal meetings to discuss unusual developments in the student's education. School information sessions should also be scheduled at regular intervals in community locations to inform interested adults about events at the school and give them the opportunity to ask questions and receive answers about the progress of individual students.

Correspondence can also be used effectively, if letters are direct and to the point, with a minimum of "in-house" language. While information of a negative sort should not be avoided, it should be balanced by letters that have positive information to convey. Another excellent general feedback device is a guidance department newsletter, sent to parents and also distributed widely throughout the community. The newsletter would include items about former students who are attending or have graduated from college or are involved in other noteworthy undertakings. There should also be announcements about testing programs, extra-curricular events, particularly those open to the public, athletic events, and the accomplishments of currently enrolled students. Guest speakers should also be employed in conveniently scheduled programs for parents and other adults to bring news of how the local school is performing in relation to others and to discuss opportunities available for students that relate to their school progress. Serious problems of individual students should be discussed privately, preferably at the home of the student.

As we become increasingly aware of the impact of out-of-school environmental conditions on school performance, and make greater efforts to manipulate that environment, the need for effective follow-up techniques is increased. One obvious example of the need for school-to-community follow-up occurs when the counselor has been instrumental in securing a part-time job for the student. The counselor would need to check with both employer and family to see if this arrangement was working out satisfactorily for all concerned, and particularly for the educational advantage of the student. For example, it may be that the job solved a family financial problem but created a new problem of the job contributing to the development of hypertension in the student that was affecting his school performance. The counselor who was following up on the case would be in a position to help correct the situation.

One example of a crucial area where follow-up is needed is college placement. High school counselors in ghetto schools have more than the normal responsibility in following up on college placement because for their clients, college enrollment, particularly at a residential campus away from home, involves serious problems of adjustment. Follow-up should take the forms of contact with the student while he is in his freshman year as well as contact with his school and parents. The counselor should serve as intermediary between the student and the college and between the student and family. There will be social problems, academic problems, and probably financial problems, regardless of how attractive the college's financial aid offer may have appeared. The timely intervention of the school counselor in any of these areas could easily spell the difference between survival or failure for the student during the first year. This is so because the counselor would be the only one in the dialogues among student, family, and college who would have good practical knowledge about all three and, consequently, he would be in the best position to harmonize the elements of all three for the best educational interests of the student.

4

....

Guidance and Behavioral Change

From the time the typical urban poor student enters school until he leaves, he is confronted with the need to make continual behavioral adaptations that exceed in degree and number those required of all but the most atypical middle-class child. In order to be successful in school, the child of the ghetto may have to make changes in family relations, aspirations, peer group relations, self-image, relations with teachers and other middle-class adults, and other typical ways of dealing with the world and its inhabitants. Behavioral changes generally require changes in how the student views himself, or how he believes others view him, or how he would like to see himself. The guidance staff has primary responsibility for assisting urban poor students in these attitudinal changes and following through with assistance in the behavioral adaptations themselves. It is critical that as the counselor assumes this role he remains sensitive to placing responsibility where it properly belongs. Generally, it will be found that the school has culpability for the problems of the student. If so, the counselor should not encourage the student to change to meet the inappropriate demands of the school. Rather, he should assist the student in reorienting the school's attitude to a more beneficial one.

We know that motivation stems from aspirational level and values and is affected by the self-concept of the individual (Daniel & Keith,

1967). We also know that the poor student must be motivated to make those behavioral changes that are necessary to his success in school. To be most effective in promoting these changes, the counselor must concentrate on structuring school experiences that allow the student to set reachable goals (Washington, 1968). The goals must be clearly delineated and agreed upon as worthwhile by both counselor and student. It is equally important that the means for achieving the goal must be made clear and agreed upon.

Because of the need that many urban poor youth have for immediate gratification for their efforts, and the greater strength that concrete rewards hold for them as opposed to the abstract sort that are generally employed in school, it is important that the first goals set by a new counseling relationship be reachable with relative ease in a short period of time. Rewards for achieving these goals should at first be as concrete as possible, gradually moving to more abstract and deferred forms. Unfortunately, this theory has most often been employed in forms that are essentially penal strategies. For example, unusually good deportment might be rewarded by release from a study hall or by allowing the student a very favorable time schedule, or even with toys or candy. This strategy is similar to the warden in the prison rewarding good behavior by making the prisoner a trustee with special privileges, or releasing him on parole before he has served his full sentence. The reason that this approach often crops up in ghetto schools is that in many ways, the school does relate to the student as a prison does to the convict. The guidance counselor should structure concrete rewards that are consistent with educational values, rather than utilizing release from negative aspects of school as rewards, since eradication of these negative features is a goal that the guidance specialist should pursue for the general good of all students.

The kinds of concrete rewards that are appropriate to employ are those that follow naturally from good school performance as beneficial results of that performance. Thus, improved behavior should be followed by improved relations with teachers and better attendance should result in better performance, other factors being equal. Improved study and application in a particular course could be rewarded by securing part-time employment of a higher order than might otherwise be expected. For example, strong application to a bookkeeping course might lead to the counselor finding the student a job involving bookkeeping in a local small business. Subsequent to achieving relatively easy, short-term goals with concrete rewards, longer term goals should be set which have successively more abstract rewards with longer periods of gratification attainment attached to them. If this procedure is successful, the counselor will find that he can eventually deal with the student in the manner most conducive to school success, with the student tolerating long-term goals that involve delayed, abstract forms of gratification. Along the way, the student will have experienced changes in self-image and aspirational level which will have affected his peer group and family relations. If the process is successful, these new evaluations and relationships will allow for strivings for academic and vocational achievement more in line with the student's innate ability than would otherwise have been the case. The way to start this process is by identifying the strengths of the student and seeing to it that he has the opportuniy to exhibit and develop these strengths in achieving meaningful goals. The process should change the usual expectation of meager results from efforts in school to more satisfying results (Daniel & Keith, 1967).

The counselor must be careful to avoid attacks on values held by the student, regardless of how destructive they may appear, if he has no compensating value to replace them. Rather than frontal attacks on inappropriate values, guidance should expose value alternatives to the person who suffers from very restricted acquaintance with a variety of value patterns (Daniel & Keith, 1967). The student must be allowed the personal freedom to choose among values. It is the task of guidance to see to it that positive school-related values have the opportunity to blossom and reach fulfillment.

It is doubtful that the student will show much interest in changing his behavior or values as a result of contact with the guidance specialist that is random and perfunctory. The counselor should start by assessing the latent potential of a student and then involving him in group guidance that indicates how the student can exploit the school for his benefit. When follow-up with individual counseling shows the student has some interest in changing behavior or values, scheduling another session in a week or two, or proposing particular strategies or goals that require delays in implementation will not do. Equally important, the counselor must prove himself consistent and absolutely reliable in his commitments to students. When he presents choices to students, these alternatives must really exist and be obtainable (J. E. Gordon, 1968). He must also be able to tolerate occasional losses in the student's impulse control and other evidences of recidivism. A final general principle in assisting or directing behavioral change in urban poor students is that the guidance specialist must be able to show the student the direct benefit to him that will result from a proposed change. Every proposal for change should be accompanied by a clear demonstration of the direct value that will accrue to the student. If such a demonstration cannot be made, the behavioral change should not be proposed.

Behavioral changes may take the forms of conforming to class discipline, where once the student was a severe behavior problem; or it may involve transforming a chronic truant into a pattern of regular attendance; or it may simply be a matter of improving a student's study habits. Whatever the case, these general principles have relevance in greater or lesser degree, to efforts of guidance specialists to effect behavioral change in urban poor children. The concept of guidance-assisted behavioral change is exemplified below.

College Guidance for High School Seniors

Much emphasis has been placed, in recent years, upon improving the rate of college attendance among the poor. High school college counselors have found several typical frustrations in accomplishing this goal. There is the problem of seemingly unrealistic goals borne by the student. The boy barely reading at the ninth grade level, with uniformly low college admission test scores and a mediocre class rank, who tells his counselor he plans to become a brain surgeon is an example of this type. The student may be far from stupid. Indeed, it may be remarkable that he has managed to survive in school at all, given the poor environmental conditions with which he must contend. Nevertheless, there is a point at which prior educational deficits accumulate in such amounts as to render the chances of recovery to the point of achieving very high level intellectual goals a very unlikely proposition (Bloom, et al., 1965). The counselor must be alert to this, and be prepared to redirect aspirations to areas that hold more likelihood of success. Then there is the high-performance student who, because of a lack of appropriate experiences and motivation, holds aspirations far below what his potential would indicate. Even if he is at the head of his class and has good test scores, this student will feel that college is only for the middle and upper class. Again, the guidance person must provide proper direction for motivation and aspiration.

Both cases are classic problems of college guidance for urban poor youth. These problems can be resolved with the introduction of behavioral change in the students. One method of promoting this change is introducing a form of reality testing activity appropriate to the particular problem. This practice can be introduced with varying levels of intensity, depending on the need. In the first case, where an unrealistically high goal (the medical profession) is the problem, it may be that a look at some advanced text in medicine might be all that is necessary, or perhaps witnessing surgery might do it. A more extreme level would involve arranging for the student to audit a biology or chemistry course at a local college. The same techniques may have the reverse effect on the student who does possess the necessary background for success but lacks the aspiration. This is to say that contact with the materials, students, and teachers of an area thought by the student to be beyond his ability, might result in a new confidence and enlarged view of the potentials for success he possesses.

If the diagnosis of an inappropriate educational goal is correct, and reality testing has had the desired effect, then the counselor must help the student find a new educational goal which is more in line with his strengths than was his previous choice. There should be as little time lag as possible between the realization that a goal is not appropriate and the search for a more feasible goal. When it is possible for the counselor to cause the two to overlap, that is even better.

The process of identifying a new goal is as important as the goal itself, for it is in this process that the necessary changes in behavior often occur. This process must *actively* involve the student, as a strongly held ambition, no matter how inappropriate, cannot be changed, or a new one substituted, by the counselor merely presenting ideas to the student who acts as a passive receptor. To return to the student with mediocre ability who wants to become a brain surgeon, the guidance specialist should present alternative goals that allow the student to simulate goal-related activities. For example, if the student has been helped to identify data processing programming as a tentative new goal, he could be taken to a local computer installation and placed in the hands of a programmer to learn about the work. Two or three days of after-school observation might prove sufficient for the student to make a fairly strong career decision. If not, the student should be allowed to continue his active experimentation for a longer period of time, depending on the wishes of the cooperating business concern. It is extremely beneficial for a student to secure part-time employment with a company operating in the field of his aspiration once the goal has been identified.

At the point where attainable goals are identified, the guidance specialist must make clear to the student what the educational requirements of the work are, both in high school preparation, and postsecondary study. Emphasis in this procedure must be on the concrete, practical aspects of training, rather than the theoretical or philosophical aspects. The same holds true for occupational analysis, where the emphasis should be on positive aspects of status, salary, and working conditions that will accrue from the work rather than an explanation of the place of data processing in American society, or its value to people.

The strengthening of appropriate educational and occupational aspirations provides the opportunity for important behavioral changes to take place. The student in this example would have learned about the importance of various phases of schooling for success in data processing, and would approach his studies with stronger motivation than could have been the case under the vague ambitions to become a brain surgeon.

The student, as well as the counselor, would be apprised of the kinds of skills required in data processing programming, as persistence in problem solving, attention to detail, and a logical, systematic approach to problems. The counselor could point out the relationships to the student's class work and related activities, and such preachments would no longer ring hollow to the student. The counselor should work with the student until the student reaches the point where he is convinced of his own ability at mastering these qualities. The result should be a better student who would stand a good chance at completion of a junior college data processing program and employment as a computer programmer.

More often than not, this type of process will forestall a student's disillusionment with education as he fails to cope with demands of academic preparation beyond his ability. Instead, behavior will be directed towards attainable goals that will reinforce his confidence in his own capabilities and the ability of the school to assist him in achieving academic and vocational success. The observable behavioral differences between the student who has set an unreasonable goal for himself and the one who has settled on an attainable one, eventually are manifested in classroom behavior, attendance, and personal involvement in utilizing the school to the best advantage.

The guidance specialist will find that the cooperation of business and professions can be secured with relative ease. The first requirement is finding out what resources are available through commercial firms, industrial firms, and professional associations. Any urban area has a multiplicity of these groups. Industrial and commerical firms, unions, and professions are all eager to cooperate with schools, particularly those in deprived areas, due to a heightened social consciousness brought on by the civil rights movement, the demands of new civil rights legislation, and their own needs for adequate manpower sources. While many firms will provide assistance on an ad hoc basis, others, such as Bell and Howell, Minnesota Mining and Manufacturing, International Business Machines, to name a few, have well-developed industrial training programs that can easily be adapted to guidance needs. Most professional associations and unions provide informational services as part of their program. These services included printed matter, films or filmstrips, and speakers. The next step would be making contact with these groups. Written contact is superior to telephoning for the initial contact. A letter on school stationery should be sent to the head of the association or the appropriate company official detailing the needs that the guidance specialist has that can be met by the firm or association. A specific request should be made, as for a person to speak on a particular subject or for a visit to a firm that would highlight certain phases of operation. The letter should also suggest specific alternate dates and indicate the general type of students who would participate. This should be done well in advance of the intended date of implementation. From that point on, follow-up by phone is recommended.

The types of groups and the beneficial involvements that can accrue from contacts with them are as follows:

1. Professional Associations: These groups represent such diverse vocations as accountants, engineers, teachers, medical doctors, pharmacists, various sales fields, actors, photographers, journalists, and many others. Representatives can be brought to the school to discuss their vocation, distribute literature and answer questions posed by students. Students particularly attracted to one field can be placed in personal contact with a representative who can offer advice and support, and probably secure part-time employment for the student.

2. Commercial and Industrial Firms: Most of the large firms in this category can do all of the above and, in addition, could provide practical experience for interested students through enrollment in their training programs by special arrangements for after-school, week-end, or summer participation. They can also provide students with the opportunity to visit the firm and receive on-site orientation to the work of the firm.

3. Labor Unions: The organization of most unions parallels the services offered by associations and business firms. In addition, particularly in the craft unions, there is the potential for entrance into skilled trades that offer more secure employment through participation in apprenticeships that can be entered after high school graduation.

As the guidance specialist develops contact with these groups, more ambitious programs can be developed. It may be that a cooperative proposal for foundation or government funding will be developed, or a particular training program established for students, or perhaps a cooperative work-study program with joint school and business sponsorship. These more elaborate practices should be accompanied by involvement of the school administrators.

Whenever possible, the guidance specialist should attempt to provide the cooperating agency with benefits for their time and efforts.

This can be done through news releases about the company's contributions to local papers, letters of gratitude, and similar devices.

The reality testing technique for the student who demonstrates strong academic promise but is a victim of a low aspirational level brought about by life in an urban slum, should be characterized by raising his aspirational level through setting and achieving short-term goals accompanied by frequent concrete reinforcements. The aim is to change his attitude from defeatism toward higher education to one of looking forward to it with hope and confidence. The first rule for counselor-client interaction is that the counselor must relate higher education to direct benefit for the student. The parents of the youngster should also be involved and shown that there are benefits to a college education that can realistically be expected, and that these benefits are attainable by the student. One excellent way to make this point is to have a college admissions officer produce a commitment for admission and financial aid for the student.

This kind of circumstance will occur only through the persistent efforts of high school guidance specialists in making college admission officers aware of the realities of urban poor society. In a day when many colleges are eagerly seeking applicants from urban ghettos, their receptivity to the advice of school guidance personnel is more favorable than ever before. To be successful in achieving this end, more than just talk may be required. The counselor may find it advantageous to make it known to college representatives that they do not intend to allow the time of students to be wasted by interviews that will result in only tenuous commitments that are often misunderstood. A system whereby counselors provide the student's records for review by the college representative prior to his meeting with the student would be advisable. Then the counselor should sit in on meetings between the two to insure that the student's interests are best served. Following the meeting, the counselor should secure written confirmation and clarification of admission and financial aid opportunities.

The establishment of close working relationships with the many colleges and universities scouring urban areas for disadvantaged academic talent, can provide the guidance specialist with the information and contacts needed to produce this type of positive, concrete reinforcement. The best environment for discussions about college is not the counselor's office nor a college admissions office, but the student's home. When seeking to entice a student into a forbidding, untried area, it is best that the environment for discussion be the most comfortable for the students and parents.

The urban environment offers great opportunity for appropriate educational reality testing situations. Almost any urban area contains a variety of institutions of higher education which allows for visits of prospective students, and often provides them with tours and the chance to talk with admissions officers and faculty, as well as college students. The experience can help to dispel many fears and misgivings about college attendance for the student. Another good experience is to involve this youngster in a loosely-structured group session with other ghetto products who are attending college in the area or have graduated from college. Just seeing such excellent role models is stimulating enough; when there is also a chance to interact on an un-hurried, fairly intimate basis, the experience can be very productive, and far more effective than anything the counselor could say. The role of the counselor in this experience should simply be to keep the dis-cussion relevant to concerns of college attendance.

The proximity of colleges to the urban ghettos also allows for the ultimate test of reality for the student — enrollment in a college course, either during the summer between the junior and senior year or in a late afternoon course during the school year. Many colleges will enroll high school students for credit, or provide special summer programs for disadvantaged students. The guidance specialist must not push the student into this, but do this only when it is clear that the student wishes it, and that he possesses the skill necessary for a reasonable chance of success in the particular course to be undertaken. Also, there must be adequate provision for feedback to the student, his parents and the guidance specialist as to course progress, so that aca-demic and emotional support can be provided as needed.

In the case of those whose entire social milieu militates against college aspiration, peer influences will play a critical role in the devel-opment of a commitment to higher education. The guidance specialist should do all he can to encourage strong peer group support for col-lege attendance. One way to do this is to develop activities that bring persons together who can be mutually reinforcing. One such device is a "college club" for high school students. Among the activities would be inviting college and professional representatives to speak to the group, visits to colleges, presenting reports on subjects relevant to col-lege attendance, and hearing from currently enrolled college students.

The counselor should then capitalize on these changes in aspira-tional level to produce behavioral changes that generally result from the student expending more energy on school work than previously in order to improve his qualifications for attending a wide range of col-leges. New books are read, new personal contacts are made among peers and school personnel, and similar changes occur as the student becomes convinced that he can dare to aspire to a college degree.

Regardless of whether the counselor is working with a student with unrealistically high goals or unrealistically low aspirations, there are several principles to which he should adhere. He must, at every step of the college guidance process, involve parents. Urban poor parents are often either apathetic or ignorant about the matter of college attendance. Even those who are optimistic about it usually fail to engage in the long-range planning that must be done if college attendance is to become a reality (Vontress, 1968). Therefore, close contact and help to parents in understanding and coping with the issue of college attendance for their children is essential. By all means, parents should be given the opportunity to meet the admission representative and visit the college. Also, it cannot be emphasized too strongly that the student's history of tenuous relations to long-term goals and symbolic rewards, requires that there be frequent concrete reinforcement during the college-searching process. Thus, official notification of admission should be solicited as soon as possible, and financial aid offers should be firm and understandable. It is also important that the counselor provide assistance to students in such matters as filling out forms properly and meeting application deadlines. The ineptitude with which such formal communications and procedures are handled by the urban poor, it should be remembered, is not due to inability (if it were, college would certainly not be feasible) but rather to the historic discomfort they associate with formal communications of any kind (Vontress, 1968). Finally, the counselor should help the student enter college without any a priori assumptions about what the student knows about college life and its demands. Such terms as "dormitory," "credit hour," "bachelor's degree" and other basic vocabulary about college will usually be completely foreign to them. The guidance specialist should be sure to see that such terms are absorbed in a systematic way when college searching begins in earnest.

Changing Hostile Behavior

Hostility in the classroom may have a number of causes. For the urban poor student, there are two main reasons. First is the need for attention from adults and peers by children accustomed to being beaten down by competition from the television set and competing peers in the home, and from large numbers of peers on the street. Many of these children settle into a pattern of getting attention from aggressive behavior in both situations and transfer this behavior to the school, where some of the same conditions exist. The second typical cause of disruptive school behavior on the part of urban poor children is the feeling of inadequacy or inability to cope with the demands of formal education.

In either case, the remedy can be found only through the cooperative efforts of the guidance specialist, teachers, parents, and significant others working with the student in ways appropriate to each. The idea is to develop a total interaction process that brings to bear a number of people, ideas and attitudes to influence the student's behavior from different directions in a pattern of dynamic interaction that involves most of the influential persons in the student's human environment (Daniel, 1967).

Conference Techniques

The case conference technique can have value in this matter. The appropriate educators and supportive school personnel should meet to discuss the manifestations and causes of the inappropriate behavior. The discussion should result in formulating some real alternatives for the student in the school setting, that have potential for satisfying the diagnosed needs of the student and also allow for opportunities for him to "blow off steam" and receive regular opportunities for the projective expression of hostility and for the understanding of these expressions by the individual and the school personnel (Krumbein, 1969). These alternatives may include opportunities for directed self-study to obtain credit for a course, rather than regular classroom participation, allowing the student and teacher to decide jointly on the outcomes that will determine a course grade, more frequent individual counseling, leaving school for one term, or whatever else seems advisable.

Parental assistance in correcting misbehavior is most meaningful when part of an overall plan involving the parents, school personnel, and the student. The process might start with a group guidance session that includes a number of parents and teachers, led by a guidance specialist. Although there should be a purpose for inviting each parent, they need not all have children expressing hostile behavior in the classroom. These periodic sessions should concentrate on the development of mutually conceived plans for guidance and instructional improvement for specific students. A second session about the same case or cases would be improved by including students who are unrelated to the parental participants, who can react to parental plans and initiatives and possibly improve them. The decision to include students at these later stages must be approved by the parents without undue pressure being exerted by the guidance specialists. It also may be advisable to include community persons at particular sessions, again, with parental approval. The time and place of meetings should be at the convenience of the parents, which may require counselors to be available on evenings or week-ends for meetings in the neighborhood of the school. The best approach would be to alternate meetings among community places, parents' homes, and the school. An occasional meeting at the home of the counselor or a teacher would also be advisable. It is important that the same parents and other adults not be continually invited to meetings. There is not enough time or personnel for that.

At times, the aggressive student might be invited to attend a meeting and discuss his program of studies, his academic problems and aspirations, and anything else he wishes to bring before the group. The description of academic problems might prove revealing not only for helping the individual, but also for adjustments that would improve education for all students in the school. The same is true for the potential contributions of other non-educators, for parents, students, and community persons can provide insights not available to school personnel. When a student is involved in developing solutions for improvements in self-defined problems, or problems identified by persons representing a number of areas of the student's life, there is a good chance of reducing the aggressive behavior that is the outward manifestation of those problems. The reason is that the student has been given the attention he probably lacks, by a group composed of persons he considers significant in varying degrees. Also, insights are provided by persons outside the school, which broaden the perspectives of the student in ways that have meanings for him that cannot generally be conveyed by his middle-class counselors and teachers.

Role Models

Another valuable spin-off from the comprehensive group guidance technique can be providing the student who is a disciplinary problem with a role model with whom he can identify. The role model can be found in the person of a fellow student who has excelled in a manner acceptable to the school, and has been a group guidance participant. The counselor should not, of course, recommend the role model to the problem student, but rather he should structure situations that supplement contact and interaction between the two at group guidance sessions and at other times. The options available for this are many, and it is best to structure several possible role model choices into these situations. Finally, the counselor should not consider obtaining a proper role model to be his exclusive task. He should present the idea to the other adults involved in the group guidance program, and they may be able to find suitable role models from either inside or outside the school.

It should be the task of the guidance specialist to see to it that the student's efforts to emulate a role model are assisted in every way possible, both inside and outside of the school. At times, this may mean interceding with a teacher to allow for some extra time out of class to participate in a community activity if that is the direction that the role identification takes, or interceding with a parent to trade time spent on household tasks for time to participate on a school athletic team. As the process of identification grows, it will require many intercessions on the student's behalf as well as continual emotional support through individual counseling.

Peer Group and Other Summary Concerns

The change from hostile to cooperative school behavior will lead to uneasy, strained peer group relations as the student desatellizes from one group and enters another. The guidance specialist should not only be available to provide the necessary support, but he should also take responsibility for marshalling others to the support of the student. This may take him out into the community to talk to an employee of the student's boys' club, his parents, new friends and old friends, and others. It may also be necessary to work out ways of improving the student's wardrobe, if that seems a requirement of unstrained participation in the new group. Certainly it will be necessary to alert teachers to the need to adopt a different approach to the student than the one that they have been accustomed to using in order to exercise control over him. There is no telling what else may be needed to support the student in his transition from aggressive to cooperative school behavior. The important thing is for the guidance specialist to remain sensitive and flexible in support of the student's needs at this critical time in his school career.

5

Guidance and Environmental Manipulation

Traditionally, when the student and school were at odds, the position of counseling and guidance was to help the student adjust to the demands of the school. Fortunately, we are now beginning to realize that guidance for the disadvantaged must not only aim to adjust the student to the school, but it must be concerned with helping the student create adjustments in the school that would be educationally useful to him, for there can be little argument about the fact that the school has not provided a very humane or useful environment for the disadvantaged. Further, guidance has begun to recognize a responsibility to extend this assistance at adapting external conditions to the student's advantage into the community and home life of the student. What we have usually asked the poor to do is cope with a school situation based on assumptions of middle-class attitudes, aspirations, skills, and home and community environment that do not exist for them. The school authorities place the poor in the illogical position of expecting them to adapt to middle-class life expectations before the conditions of that life become available to them in either their psychological or material form.

The guidance specialist must assume responsibility for assisting the student in identifying and removing environmental obstacles to academic success that are found within the school (internal environment) and in the student's environment outside the school (external environment). There are two contrasting concepts of the proper role of the counselor in assisting in corrective manipulation of obstructive conditions to the best educational performance of urban poor students in either environmental situation. Patterson (1969) contends that it is not, nor should it be, a matter in which the counselor alone works with an individual student. Rather he sees environmental manipulation as a task shared by the total school staff and societal agencies appropriate to the task. He sees these groups as concerned with meeting the needs of all students in an organized, predictable fashion. This approach takes the forms of special classes, remedial and tutoring programs, and so on. Gordon (1967), on the other hand, sees the proper way to assist the student in alterations in the environment stemming from a personal partnership between the counselor and the student. His position becomes clear in this extract from his writings:

> I see the guidance worker as a partner with the student in the struggle to make appropriate use of those factors in the environment that best facilitate development and to change those factors that retard or distort wholesome growth. I see counselor and student together, utilizing the natural reinforcers of the environment to consolidate desired behaviors . . . I see them utilizing the abrasive and negative factors in the environment not to discourage or depress, but to stimulate resistance and change. I see the natural identification, involvement and commitment of these two human beings to the development of a more humane environment. . . . Such an approach would seem to be particularly appropriate for work with disadvantaged youngsters since it is against them that the environment is most heavily stacked.

In a later paper, Gordon (1969) elaborated on his earlier position:

> The guidance specialist's principal function would be . . . environmental manipulation. Much of what hangs kids up is not internal to them. . . . Interaction with the environment is a primary determinant of what anyone can become. . . . He must be concerned with institutional modifications as a route to changing the youngster's behavior. . . . The counselor may need to be prominently identified with the courses, the problems and the conditions important to those with whom he works.

Gordon's view of the counselor as catalyst and partner with the student in manipulating internal and external environmental conditions should be adopted for use with urban poor students rather than the more traditional position supported by Patterson. It should be clear to any observer of inner-city education that traditional guidance approaches such as Patterson's have failed, and must give way to more activist approaches, as the one advocated by Gordon, in which the counselor assumes a greater responsibility for helping the individual not only cope with the environment, but alter it as well. This approach is particularly well-suited to urban poor students, for whom the person-to-person verbal process with counselors has had little impact in producing important behavioral or environmental changes. It is much more important for the counselor to show that he can produce results for the student. Rapport and confidence will most likely be established with these youngsters in proportion to the ability of the guidance specialist to get things done, and even more important, in showing the student what he himself can do to beneficially alter his own environment. This position has as a primary assumption the reversal of the traditional view that the locus of academic and adjustive difficulties is in the student, rather than the conditions to which the student is asked to adapt. Instead, the view must be that though individual verbal counseling is necessary, the more important task is structuring social, economic, and educational changes for the student that will lessen the effects of disadvantagement and increase his ability to cope with school (J. E. Gordon, 1968).

Dividing environmental manipulation into internal and external categories is a theoretical construct useful only for explanatory purposes. The real life challenges that will confront the counselor attempting to aid students by helping them alter their environment will usually involve both environmental dimensions. The example chosen to elaborate on environmental manipulation makes no distinction between internal and external emphases as would be the case in reality.

Altering Internal Environmental Conditions

Alteration or manipulation of conditions within the school will probably involve the counselor with most of the school staff — administrators, teachers, clerks, custodial employees, and others. Although it is a reasonable assumption that they are all generally committed to the best interests of the students, we know that they all may view what is "best" through a different prism, particularly when the newer or more unusual aims of students conflict with status positions of school personnel, and their obligations for internalized organizational responsibility, as school housekeeping tasks and following set procedures. This problem might be dealt with on a one-to-one basis or through a case conference, in which it is demonstrated that the needs of a particular student demand restructuring or at least re-thinking traditional roles and relationships on the part of school personnel.

The most obvious intervention of the counselor in the classroom would be to remove a student from a class where the relationship between the student and teacher is destructive to the student's educational progress, and place the student with a teacher who can better meet his needs. This will require the guidance specialist to know the teachers as well as he does the students. The counselor must also be sensitive to the need to change a student's class schedule in order to remove him from classroom contact with peers who prevent him from performing at his best in class. Other types of internal environmental alterations would be modifying a student's time schedule to allow him to start school earlier or later, as required by the nature of his problem, to arrange for the student to receive individual tutoring or an independent study course when that seems advisable, and similar interventions. At times it may be necessary to intercede with the principal to allow a student or group of students to pursue a unique interest that may not be directly related to the standard school program. This may be carried to the point where the counselor, at the behest of his clients, will instigate discussions with the administration designed to radically change existing programs or create new ones that will better serve the educational and psycho-social needs of urban poor students.

Again, the case conference technique provides an excellent vehicle to achieve the desired end. The sensitivity of teachers or administrators must be regarded in this. If it seems advisable for a student to be transferred from one teacher to another, the guidance specialist must present this in a manner that is not disparaging to the present teacher of the student, if this is at all possible. Where it seems clear that the teacher's thinking must be reoriented for the good of all of his students, this should be done apart from the formal case conference setting. The counselor should also be prepared to assume the administrative obligations involved in these internal changes.

Guidance personnel must expect to be at odds with some school people from time to time. Imagine the attitude of the typical school janitor who is asked to heat the building an hour before the accustomed time, or to clean rooms an hour after the normal school closing time. School clerks who find that they are asked to maintain additional sets of records resulting from new guidance procedures or methods of dealing with outside visitors would present a similar problem. The most powerful opponents to internal environmental manipulation would generally be the teachers. Therefore, it behooves the counselor, in the best interests of his clients, to proceed with care when dealing with teachers who, it must be recognized, affect the educational process and total development of the student as much or more than a counselor possibly could. The chief task when dealing with the administration will be convincing the principal that the procedures or changes to be effected have a sound basis and will not undermine the operation of the school. A careful plan that assures the smooth integration of an internal change for one or more students should be presented along with the request for change. Objections raised by the administration should be debated and resolved on a mutually agreeable basis, which may involve adjustments in the plans of the counselor. It would be better to make some slight modifications than alienate the administration to the general approach of internal environmental manipulation.

None of the foregoing should be construed to mean that the counselor must be timid or vacillating in his relations with staff members who are counter-productive to the student's education. The guidance specialist must always keep foremost in his mind that he is working toward creating a more humane school environment for the disadvantaged learner. This can best be done by helping the staff to gain new insights on their roles. For example, they should view their success in terms of how well they have helped students to reach their maximum potential, rather than how well they have held to arbitrary standards of excellence in their classes. However, it may also be necessary, at times, to draw the lines of battle with teachers or administrators holding on to elements of penal psychology in the school, or regulations and standards more suited to different students of a bygone era.

The first rule for relating to other staff members is to involve them as fully as possible in the rationale and development of environmental alterations. They cannot be left to feel like obstructions to progress or neutral pawns to be manipulated at the caprice of the counselor. The guidance specialist must recognize that he cannot produce and implement important adaptations for the student by himself. He can initiate and make others aware of the needs for adaptations, but in the last analysis it will be the teacher or the administration or someone else who may be the key person to the success of an alteration in some aspect of the school program or its supportive services. The counselor is, in a real sense, dependent on these other staff members, and should make this fact apparent to them. Initiation of changes should be followed by the counselor's being concerned not only for the adjustment of the student in a new situation, but also for the problems that may have appeared for the staff due to the change. A willingness to actively assist in alleviating new pressures should characterize this involvement on the part of the guidance specialist. Finally, the counselor must always stand ready to move continually in to support new relationships and adaptations and, when necessary, terminate a change that has proven ineffective.

Altering External Environmental Conditions

The point has been made that the guidance function must extend beyond the school, for in the urban poor community, conditions may exist that render the student, regardless of how willing he may be, incapable of benefiting from the school program. The counselor must obtain information about the environmental forces affecting school performance. This can only be done by the counselor spending time out in the community with parents, social agencies and, most important, with the students themselves. A school personnel organization that allows guidance specialists the time for this is essential. Environmental changes cannot be initiated or supported by guidance personnel unless these changes are understood and accepted by the significant persons in the community who have an effect on the student's life. Thus, it is important that the guidance specialist not attempt to promote alterations before a stable relationship has been established with the others needed to make it work. Even when this has been accomplished, the counselor should proceed with caution. The initial changes should be minimal and carry very strong possibilities of success. Gradually, as the counselor becomes more capable of dealing with particular persons outside the school, and the student in his community environment, more far-reaching changes can be attempted.

The guidance specialist must clearly understand that he has serious limitations in influencing external environmental changes, in contrast to his position within the school. He must recognize that he is usually dealing with deep-seated modes of behavior that do not easily lend themselves to quick change, even when the student's problems demand immediate alteration. The range of environmental manipulations that the counselor will generally be most competent in affecting include securing part-time employment for the student, arranging for food and clothing from welfare sources, and convincing parents that continuing in high school or going on to college is better than any other course of action for their child.

It will be much more difficult for the counselor to provide conditions that will allow a student to dissociate himself from a neighborhood gang. The same is true for efforts at arranging for home conditions more conducive to doing homework, regular hours of retiring at night, and awaking in the morning, and other patterns of behavior that increase potential for school success. The reason is that the former examples do not require the student or those he is personally involved with to change their life styles to any significant extent. In the latter cases, however, the first example demands a change in a habitual pattern of relations encouraged by the mere juxtaposition of people as well as the very real social and physical pressures against change. The second example asks a hard-pressed parent to reorder a home environment that may already be under great strain into one perceived to be even more inconvenient. In a milieu that is generally uncertain and encourages one to live for the gratification of the moment, it requires quite a bit of encouragement for them to alter the small comforts they are able to snatch for the sake of a long-term, uncertain goal.

Due to these circumstances, the counselor is well advised to first alter those conditions that do not require changes in strongly entrenched modes of behavior. Ideally, the more difficult alterations should be preceded by successful manipulation of the less upsetting types. If the counselor has been successful in obtaining an after-school job for the student that is acceptable to the student and parents and results in alleviating a family financial crisis, it will be much easier for the counselor to convince parents to have certain quiet hours, to provide a place for the youngster to study, and generally improve those home conditions that may have an effect on his education.

An Example of Environmental Manipulation

The illustration chosen to underscore the necessary marriage of internal and external environmental manipulation in meeting the total needs of the student for environmental adjustment is a typical human dilemma of ghetto life — the bright fifteen-year-old girl who has had a child out of wedlock and wishes to finish school and build a successful life for herself and her child.

Almost all of the conditions of her environment militate against accomplishing this goal. Indeed, the fact that so many girls in this circumstance attempt to finish high school and learn useful occupations is a tribute to the indomitable will that is characteristic of so many impoverished young women. Although the unwed teen-age mother is not stigmatized in the ghetto to the same extent as would be true in most other segments of American society, her condition does set her apart from her peers, and renders her more vulnerable to their assaults. The girl's father will generally be outraged, if he happens to still live with his family, while the mother will be more accepting of the event, even as she bemoans the added burden of another person to care for and support. If the girl's mother agrees to care for the baby while her daughter goes to school, this not only places an additional strain on the mother's time and financial resources, but also alters the mother-daughter relationship in a way that requires the daughter to be much more beholden to the parent than in the past. This places a new burden on the normally tenuous family life of the urban poor. The usual teen-age life is denied to the girl, and even knowing that the cause for this is of her own doing will not lessen the regret and frustration this will cause. There will also be the added problem of having to care for the baby after school, which added to the time spent on whatever social life is available to her (and is much needed), will leave little time or energy for study. Finally, there will be the handicaps to good school performance that result from excessive absences and tardiness resulting from the need to supplement the mother's efforts at caring for the child in the emergencies common to child-rearing, as well as the need to occasionally relieve the mother when she is not able or willing to extend the care that the baby will need.

In addition to the pressures that lead to school failure and early leaving experienced by all urban poor youth, then, the unwed mother has these additional impediments to success. Here, indeed, is fertile ground for environmental manipulation. The involvement of the counselor might start when tardiness has caused the first period teacher to resort to requesting that he resolve the problem or arrange to have the student dropped from that course. If the counselor had not already done so, as should have been the case, a first step at this point would be to inquire into the conditions which may have given rise to the tardiness. Talking to the student should uncover the fact of the baby, if guidance records had not already revealed that fact to the counselor. This determination should be followed by a home visit to discuss the problem with mother and daughter together.

The interview should not dwell upon threats to drop the student from the course, but rather should stress the benefits that graduation will bring to all members of the family and ways of working out solutions to the problem at hand. The counselor might agree to have the girl's class transferred from the first period to the last period, if that would be compatible with the school's course offerings and the girl's class schedule. If that course is not offered at a period beyond the girl's last presently scheduled class, the counselor might arrange an independent study course for the student through the case conference procedure. The possibility of allowing the student to continue to come to class late should not be overlooked if other alternatives seem unlikely. Many teachers who would be informed of the circumstances behind the tardiness would relent and allow the student to come in late from time to time. Some of the missed time could be made up by meeting with the teacher during a preparation period, or some other out-of-class time. Solutions might also be reached by enlisting the aid of neighborhood mothers who could lend a hand when needed, or keep an eye on the family schedule.

Excessive absences present a more serious academic problem and one that is more difficult to solve. It may be possible for the counselor to arrange for the baby to be cared for on an irregular basis by a local welfare agency, or if the child is old enough, enrollment in a local "Head Start" program might be the answer. Investigation might also find that certain women in the neighborhood regularly care for the children of working mothers, and possibly would agree to care for this child, when the necessity arose. If the solution to the absence problem involved additional expense to the student and her family, the counselor should tie into the arrangement an opportunity to acquire the necessary funds without jeopardizing school attendance or home responsibilities. One method would be to arrange for a job in the school lunchroom, or perhaps a financial grant from a social service agency or local businesses. Still another solution would be to find a full-time job for the mother that would allow for regular employment of a baby-sitter. There is also the possibility of arranging with teachers to allow missed work to be made up at home, while the girl is caring for the child. If there are quite a few girls with babies to care for who wish to finish high school, as may well be the case, the counselor should work to have the school hire a para-professional to care for the babies at the school.

The obvious answer to the need for peer group and emotional support would be for the guidance specialist to conduct group guidance sessions with these girls. At these meetings, the unwed mothers would have the opportunity to exchange information and views and, with the help of the counselor, arrive at solutions to general problems faced by all of them. Some sessions should be devoted to hearing from adult women who were unwed mothers at high school age, for their advice and experiences would provide valuable information to the student. Securing these women as speakers would not be difficult for the counselor with good community contacts. All that would be required is for him to mention the idea to the key communicators he knows in the community with the request that those adult women who had raised children out of wedlock and were willing to contribute to the group guidance should call him. These persons should be screened by the counselor to insure a balance of role models, an awareness of the attitudes of these women toward receiving criticism, and their view of their own roles. At times, the information will lead the counselor to not allow some of these women to participate. Another type of outside resource person would be social workers connected with homes for unwed mothers, adoption agencies, and similar institutions. These persons are easily available through contact with the appropriate agency and are generally eager for the kind of experience presented by this group guidance technique.

The guidance specialist should also be prepared to make referrals to agencies that provide the kind of help these students would typically need. These would include clinics specializing in child care, marriage counseling and the like. After a time, girls who have built up strong peer support and are doing well should be deactivated from the guidance group. The guidance specialist should, however, maintain contact with them not only so as to continue to be of service, but also to have them as future resource persons to the newer members of the guidance group.

Throughout the extended group guidance the counselor should be sensitive to opportunities to improve the environment of the clients. At times this may require the counselor to support an organized effort on the part of the girls to change a school regulation that has particularly adverse effects on them. At other times, it will mean going to see a girl's parents to plead a case for her, perhaps in the company of other members of the guidance group. There will also be opportunities for the group, led by the counselor or by one of the girls, to lobby for improved safety in the community or better play facilities for their children. In all this, the guidance specialist should play an active role.

The main point in this and other cases is that the counselor must interact with the student, parent, and teachers, presenting a number of viable alternatives to each that will eventually result in solution of the problem and then help make the selected alternative a reality. The benefits of dealing with the guidance specialist should be immediate and real. The counselor should not become involved in pushing for a solution if this outcome cannot be reasonably expected; for a lot of talk that produces no concrete benefit for the poor people involved will only reinforce existing impressions of the ineffectiveness of social institutions to meet their needs. Telling them that they should simply strive to overcome obstacles because the long-term goal is worth it, will usually be received with apathy, for their problems are real and they are immediate, and they probably have never experienced the fruition of such a long-term benefit as the counselor is presenting to them.

The circumstances requiring a counselor to stay completely out of a problem because he has no viable approach to beneficial environmental manipulation should be rare. There are generally an enormous range of resources available both within the school and in the community for the guidance specialist to utilize, if he is energetic and resourceful enough. The success of environmental manipulation depends not only on the ability of the counselor to identify a solution, but also on his ability to develop an active working partnership with the persons involved in the various aspects of solution. The guidance specialist should not, and most often cannot, effect these changes alone. He needs the help of his clients in both developing plans for solution and taking responsibilty for implementing the necessary environmental changes.

The guidance specialist who becomes active in the areas of environmental manipulation will find himself often running afoul of existing regulations and customary modes of organization and behavior both within the school and in the community. An excellent rationale to buttress him when this happens is to remember that the status quo has proven ineffective in meeting the educational needs of the deprived youngsters populating America's urban ghettos. It would be a very insensitive person, indeed, who would attempt to block experiments at environmental manipulation on the grounds that they would be disturbing established procedures. In the last analysis, the blend of internal and external environmental manipulation can gradually move people and institutions to acquire the flexibility needed to better serve all of their clients.

6

....

A Guidance Specialist for
Urban Poor Students

The persons who presently fill the guidance counselor positions in American schools have had their undergraduate training either in education or one of the subjects taught in the schools, and then, after a period of teaching, and completion of the graduate training that qualified them, were appointed as counselors. The master's degree in guidance and counseling or the pattern of graduate courses required for a counseling certificate, generally contain a preponderance of courses concerned with techniques of counseling, identifying and treating emotional disorders, and a strong dose of psychological theory. This is supplemented by one or two courses that deal with the topics of test interpretation, academic appraisal, identification and utilization of community resources, group guidance techniques, presenting occupational information, and similar matters vital to helping urban poor students. The realities of conditions in the inner-city schools, with their unfavorable counselor-client ratios, lack of adequate physical facilities, transient professional staff and student population, and similar problems, demand a reversal of the usual course priorities in training counselors. The unhurried, careful techniques of psychological therapy are of little use in such a situation, and these verbal techniques have not helped to stem a national school dropout rate of approximately one-third of all high school entrants, with considerably higher rates in the urban slums (Bloom, et al., 1965).

Counselors receiving such training quite naturally interpret their roles in line with the content of that education. A survey of elementary school counselor's role perception (Moore, 1969) revealed that they saw their main functions being: (1) consulting with pupils, teachers, principals, and others, (2) individual counseling, and (3) acting as a resource person in appraisal, consultation, and referral needs. The counselor who views his role in these verbal, essentially passive dimensions, will not be of optimum value in the schools of the urban poor. These procedures do not lend themselves to direct action and rapid alleviation of immediate problems. Further, they place the counselor in the role of a quasi-clinical psychologist, which most are not equipped to be, even though the bulk of their training has deceived them into feeling that they are adequately prepared for this.

Views on the Role of the Guidance Specialist for the Urban Poor

It is important to recognize that most urban poor children who need help and are willing to place their trust in a school counselor are hoping to find "an effective advocate who [can] change things instantly, even magically" (Blodgett & Green, 1966). In such cases, praise, promises, inspiration, and understanding, whether couched in directive or non-directive terms, does not meet the expectations of the student. Again, Edmund Gordon (1967) provides instructive clarification. He resolves the conflict between the traditional biases of school counseling and the guidance needs of urban poor students as follows:

> I see no alternative but to take the emphasis off the counseling relationship and place the emphasis on guidance as a process taking place in the continuum between directed and supported involvement and independent behavioral commitment. In this process, I see the guidance specialist and the student continually involved in behavioral and environmental manipulation to achieve specified behavioral ends.

Other authorities who recognize the same problem of the relevance of current counseling practice to the needs of the urban poor, propose different solutions. Patterson (1969) supports the use of a variety of guidance specialists — counselors, specialists in testing and evaluation, occupational information specialists, job placement experts and college admissions specialists, to name a few. In this organizational structure, the counselor would be free to really counsel. This is to say that he would have the time to engage in extended and intensive verbal therapy. The New York City Schools' More Effective Schools project called for "guidance teams to work with both children and parents. These teams would include teachers, a psychiatric consultant, social workers, and guidance counselors" (Crow, et al., 1966). Amos and Grambs (1968) recommend providing disadvantaged youth with one familiar figure in the school who will personalize their relations with the school staff, so that the student is not lost in the shuffle or put on the familiar "conveyor belt of impersonal referral procedures." In a piece written after the one quoted above, Gordon (1969) provides a conceptual framework for his idea of guidance in slum schools, by characterizing his ideal guidance specialist as a "pupil ombudsman" who would be available to protect the student against whatever adversities might appear to block educational progress. He further speculates that perhaps this person should be taken out of the organizational structure of the school and placed in some organizational or administrative relationship with the community.

The Student's Advocate

As Patterson suggests, more experts devoted to individual guidance specialties are needed, whether they work in teams or in some other organizational framework. However, the most crucial need is to provide the student with an effective advocate, an ombudsman, if you will, as recommended by Gordon. This advocacy should extend to anything within the environment of the student that may affect his school performance. Such a role would demand aptitudes in many areas. The advocate should be skilled in the identification and utilization of resources both inside and outside of the school. This does not only mean having a directory of community agencies to refer to and a list of particularly able and willing teachers and others who could be called upon for special services. It goes beyond this to the ability of the counselor to recognize the potential for community and school service to fill existing needs that lies within ancillary public agencies, private enterprises, and particular individuals. Further, he must have the ability to bring these services into action for the student's benefit. This may mean getting a local politician to see to it that a free lunch program is expanded rather than discontinued, or getting the local public librarian to establish meetings with students interested in learning more about the uses of the library, or convincing local businessmen to contribute to a fund that will provide free school supplies to students who cannot afford to buy them.

The same skill at identifying and mobilizing help must be exerted within the school. Particular teachers, students, para-professionals, and administrators should be identified and utilized in accordance with their special attributes, that would include avocational as well as professional skills. Thus, an English teacher who happened to be an excellent seamstress, might be asked to help a girl with mending her clothes, or a biology teacher who runs a boys' camp in the summer might be asked to take on one or two boys from the school at reduced rates or for no payment at all.

The student's advocate would, of necessity, find himself at odds with faculty or administration from time to time. This is so because if he truly is to serve as the advocate of the student this will involve opposing teachers or administrators about traditional practices judged to be harmful to the best interests of the student. To illustrate this point, we can take the case of the teacher who has a strict requirement that term papers not submitted by the deadline date are not accepted and a failing grade for that project is issued to the dilatory student. When the student brings this problem to the advocate, the first responsibility of the advocate would be to determine if there is any justification for intervening in the matter. If it seems to be simply a matter of the student wanting to see how much he could get away with, the matter ought to proceed no further, and the student should suffer the consequences of his behavior. If, however, there are legitimate mitigating circumstances, whether they be a case of little sister ripping up half of the report, or a power failure that kept the apartment dark the evening before the report was due, or any other plausible circumstance, the advocate ought to pursue the matter for the student. This means pressuring the teacher to set aside her rule in recognition of the frequent obstructions to education that are part of the student's out-of-school environment and the mission of the teacher to help the student succeed, not simply act as a monitor of his efforts. When confronted with the argument that this would not be fair to the other students who must abide by the regulation, there would be two possible answers: 1) The rule has shown itself to have worked an undue hardship on one student and therefore, should be modified or discarded for all students. 2) The advocate is presently concerned with the immediate welfare of one human being who needs help, and questions of a general philosophical nature have no place in the matter if they can possibly work to the detriment of the client at this point in time.

What real power can the advocate exert in this case or others? The question would partially be answered by the role definition assigned to him in the organizational structure. His skill at manipulating the participants in this struggle would be equally important. When the preponderance of power is with the opposition, enlarging the scope of conflict to include others who will serve to redress the balance of power is a good approach. This may result in bringing the issue to the attention of the principal. If the principal agrees with the teacher, the advocate might call the matter to the attention of a community leader or a college professor working with the school, or an official of a school-related citizens' organization, or a school board member; anyone who can add strength and support to the student's cause. In this way, the scope of conflict is broadened to the advantage of the student. It would be rare indeed if the administration or a teacher wishing to punish a student, would attempt to broaden the scope of conflict outside of the school. They are generally committed to keeping it as narrow as possible in order to avoid controversy and unpleasant publicity. The result of this tactic will most often be to the benefit of the student.

The potential for conflict built into this model of the student's advocate leads to the conclusion that the position should be administratively and physically located outside of the school. This is to say that the advocate should not report to the building principal or director of guidance at the school where his clients are enrolled. Rather, he should be responsible to the central office department of the school system that has guidance responsibilities for all the schools within the district, and the administrative head of students' advocates ought to report directly to the district's board of education. The advocate would still have responsibility for coordinating with and informing appropriate persons within the school to which his clients are assigned. This would not only clarify his unique relationships to the school and its students, but it would also strengthen the advocate's ability to function effectively as an aid to both the students' behavioral adaptation and environmental manipulation, while also having an impact on creating more humane and educationally productive practices in the school.

The advocate would span the two areas of environment that effect the student's education (school and community) by being physically located in the community. His office might be in a storefront, an office building or an apartment close to the school he serves. Thus, while retaining his stature and effectiveness as a professional educator, he would be adding the new dimension of being a representative in and of the community served by the school. Finally, physical location in the community would strengthen the advocate's ability to serve as a role model for altering behavior of students who often view the school and the professionals within it as somewhat unreal figures, divorced from the "real" world as they know it.

The Student's Advocate and Other Guidance Specialists

The role of the student's advocate is clearly designed for the purposes of assisting students in altering their behavior in ways that will be more conducive to success in school and assisting them in the manipulation of environmental obstacles to school success. Urban poor students are particularly in need of such services, but they also need specialized support in other areas of guidance. They need the help of specialists who can assist them in making career plans, diagnose learning problems and make interpretations of standardized test results and recommendations based on those results in line with the characteristics and needs of the individual student. Specialists in these areas should each have a clearly defined role in the guidance organization of the school.

The function of "counseling," defined as regular, intensive, verbal interactions with the student, should be assumed by the advocate, who would be free of responsibilities for testing, discipline, and so forth. In order for the advocate to be effective, he would need to have a very close working relationship with the other guidance specialists who serve within the school. The team of guidance specialists operating within the school would be performing the tasks of collecting the data that would be necessary adjuncts to the successful performance of the advocate's task. Although the relationship should be recognized in the formal organizational structure of the school, the success of this arrangement will primarily rest on the ability of the student's advocate to make it work through his skill at interpersonal relations and the use of data and resources provided by guidance specialists within the school.

BIBLIOGRAPHY

Amos, W. E., "The Nature of Disadvantaged Youth," in Amos and Grambs (Eds.), *Counseling the Disadvantaged Youth,* Englewood Cliffs, New Jersey: Prentice-Hall, 1968, pp. 13–29.

Amos, W. E. and Grambs, J. D. (Eds.), *Counseling the Disadvantaged Youth,* Englewood Cliffs, New Jersey: Prentice-Hall, 1968.

Aubrey, R. F., "Misapplication of Therapy Models to School Counseling," *Personnel and Guidance Journal,* 1969, 48, 273–278.

Barclay, L., "The Home Visit," in Kontos, P. G. and Murphy, J. J. (Eds.), *Teaching Urban Youth,* New York: John Wiley, 1967, pp. 215–220.

Bernstein, A., *The Education of Urban Populations,* New York: Random House, 1967.

Bernstein, B., "Social Class and Linguistic Development: A Theory of Social Learning," in Halsey, A. H., Floud, J. and Anderson, C. A. (Eds.), *Education, Economy and Society,* New York: The Free Press, 1961, pp. 288–314.

Blocker, C. E. and Richardson, R. C., Jr., "Teaching and Guidance Go Together," *Junior College Journal,* 1968, 39 (3) 14–16.

Blodgett, E. and Green, R. L., "A Junior High School Group Counseling Program," *Journal of Negro Education,* 1966, 35 (1) 11–17.

Bloom, B., Davis, A. and Hess, R., *Compensatory Education for Cultural Deprivation,* New York: Holt, Rinehart & Winston, 1965.

Brookover, W. B., et al., "Self-concept of Ability and School Achievement," in Miller, H. L. (Ed.), *Education for the Disadvantaged,* New York: The Free Press, 1967, pp. 64–67.

Bruner, J. S., *Toward a Theory of Instruction,* New York: W. W. Norton, 1966.

Butler, A. L., "Will Head Start be a False Start?" in Miller, H. L. (Ed.), *Education for the Disadvantaged,* New York: The Free Press, 1967.

Cloward, R. A. and Jones, J. A., "Social Class: Education Attitudes and Participation," in Passow, A. H. (Ed.), *Education in Depressed Areas,* New York: Teachers College, Columbia University, 1963, pp. 190–216.

Cody, J. J., "Appraisal of Disadvantaged Youth," in Amos and Grambs (Eds.), *Counseling the Disadvantaged Youth,* Englewood Cliffs, New Jersey: Prentice-Hall, 1968, pp. 30–53.

Cottle, W. C., "Counseling the School Dropout," in Amos and Grambs (Eds.), *Counseling the Disadvantaged Youth,* Englewood Cliffs, New Jersey: Prentice-Hall, 1968, pp. 190–205.

Crow, L. D., Murray, W. I. and Smythe, H. I., *Educating the Culturally Disadvantaged Child,* New York: David McKay, 1966.

Daniel, K. B. and Keith, J. A., "Revising Guidance Practices: An Integrative Process," in Cowles, M. (Ed.), *Perspectives in the Education of Disadvantaged Children,* Cleveland: World Publishing, 1967, pp. 213–236.

Duncan, J. A. and Gozda, G. M., "Significant Content of Group Counseling Sessions with Culturally Deprived Ninth Grade Students," *Personnel and Guidance Journal,* 1967, 46, 11–16.

Fagan, E. R., "The Disadvantaged as a Collective," *Phi Delta Kappan,* 1968, XLIX, 396–398.

Feingold, S. N., "Presenting Educational and Occupational Information to the Disadvantaged," in Amos and Grambs (Eds.), *Counseling the Disadvantaged Youth,* Englewood Cliffs, New Jersey, Prentice-Hall, 1968, pp. 256–290.

Fishman, J. A., Deutsch, M., Kogan, L., North R. and Whiteman, M., "Guidelines for Testing Minority Group Children," in Passow, A. H., Goldberg, M. and Tannenbaum, A. J. (Eds.), *Education of the Disadvantaged,* New York: Holt, Rinehart & Winston, 1967, pp. 155–169.

Gordon, E. W., "The Socially Disadvantaged Student: Implications for the Preparation of Guidance Specialist," in College Entrance Examination Board, *Preparing School Counselors in Educational Guidance,* New York: College Board, 1967, pp. 67–68.

————, "Counseling the Disadvantaged: Avenues to Effectiveness," *CAPS Capsule,* 1969, 2 (2) 3–9.

Gordon, J. E., "Counseling the Disadvantaged Boy," in Amos and Grambs (Eds.), *Counseling the Disadvantaged Youth,* Englewood Cliffs, New Jersey, Prentice-Hall, 1968, pp. 119–168.

Gottlieb, D., "Poor Youth Do Want to be Middle Class But It's Not Easy," *Personnel & Guidance Journal,* 1967, 46, 117–122.

Grande, P. P., "Attitudes of Counselors and Disadvantaged Students Toward School Guidance," *Personnel & Guidance Journal,* 1968, 46, pp. 889–892.

Gross, E., "Counselors Under Fire: Youth Opportunities Centers," *Personnel & Guidance Journal,* 1969, 47, 404–409.

Hechinger, F. M., "Curtains for Higher Horizons," in Miller, H. L. (Ed.), *Education for the Disadvantaged,* New York: The Free Press, 1967, pp. 168–169.

Henderson, G., "Role Models for Lower Class Negro Boys," *Personnel & Guidance Journal,* 1967, 46, 6–10.

Hoffer, E., *The Ordeal of Change,* New York: Harper & Row, 1952.

Kaplan, B. A., "Issues in Educating the Culturally Disadvantaged," *Phi Delta Kappan,* 1963, 45, 70–76.

Katz, I., "Academic Motivation and Equal Educational Opportunity," *Harvard Educational Review,* 1968, 38, 54–65.

Keach, E. T., Fulton, R. and Gardner, W. E. (Eds.), *Education and Social Crisis,* New York: John Wiley, 1967.

Kozol, J., "Halls of Darkness: In the Ghetto Schools," *Harvard Educational Review,* 1967, 37, 379–407.

Krumbein, E., "Wanted: A Humane School Environment," in Bruno, H. T. (Ed.), *A Quandary in Education,* Winnetka, Illinois: New Trier Township High School District #203, 1969.

Loretan, J. O. and Umans, S., *Teaching the Disadvantaged,* New York: Teachers College, Columbia University, 1966.

Margolin, J., "The Mental Health of the Disadvantaged," in Amos and Grambs (Eds.), *Counseling the Disadvantaged Youth,* Englewood Cliffs, New Jersey: Prentice-Hall, 1968, 80–100.

Mauch, J. E., "Breaking Tradition Forces School-Community Ties," *Phi Delta Kappan,* 1969, L, 270–273.

Moore, L. H., "Elementary School Guidance: The Search For Identity," *Counselor Education and Supervision,* 1969, 8, 213–219.

Newsfront, *Phi Delta Kappan,* 1969, LI, 223–227.

Niemeyer, J. H., "Home-school Interaction," in Schreiber, D. (Ed.), *Profile of the School Dropout,* New York: Vintage Books, 1968, pp. 349–365.

Orem, R. C., "Language and the Culturally Disadvantaged," in Amos and Grambs (Eds.), *Counseling the Disadvantaged Youth,* Englewood Cliffs, New Jersey: Prentice-Hall, 1968, pp. 101–118.

Owens, R. G. and Steinhoff, C. R., "Strategies for Improving Inner-City Schools," *Phi Delta Kappan,* 1969, L, 259–263.

Patterson, C. H., "Associations Aroused by Dr. Gordon," *CAPS Capsule,* 1969, 2 (2) 10–17.

Pearson, R., "Working with the Disadvantaged Groups," in Amos and Grambs (Eds.), *Counseling the Disadvantaged Youth,* Englewood Cliffs, New Jersey: Prentice-Hall, 1968, pp. 54–79.

Pitcher, E. G., "An Evaluation of the Montessori Method in Schools for Young Children," in Miller, H. L. (Ed.), *Education for the Disadvantaged.* New York: The Free Press, 1967, pp. 153–160.

Ravitz, M., "The Role of the School in the Urban Setting," in Passow, A. H. (Ed.), *Education in Depressed Areas,* New York: Teachers College, Columbia University, 1963, pp. 6–23.

Riessman, F., *The Culturally Deprived Child,* New York: Harper & Row, 1962.

Rosenthal, R. and Jacobsen, L., *Pygmalion in the Classroom,* New York: Holt, Rinehart & Winston, 1968.

Schindler-Rainman, E., "The Poor and the PTA," *The PTA Magazine,* 1967, 61 (8) 4–7.

Schwab, D., "Underestimation of Culturally Deprived Youth," in Wisniewski, R. (Ed.), *New Teachers in Urban Schools*, New York: Random House, 1968, pp. 113–138.

Smallenburg, C. and H. W., "When Students Seek Counseling," *PTA Magazine*, 1968, 62 (6) 27–29.

Tannenbaum, A. J., "Dropout or Diploma: A Socio-educational Analysis of Early Withdrawal," in Passow, A. H., Goldberg, M. and Tannenbaum, A. J. (Eds.), *Education of the Disadvantaged*, New York: Holt, Rinehart & Winston, 1967, pp. 423–438.

Terrel, G., Durkin K. & Wiesley, M., "Social Class and the Nature of the Incentive in Discrimination Learning," *Journal of Abnormal Social Psychology*, 1959, (59) 270–272.

Vontress, C. E., "Counseling Negro Students for College," *Journal of Negro Education*, 1968, 37, 37–44.

Walz, G. R., "Derivations on Disadvantagedness," *CAPS Capsule*, 1969, 2 (2) 13–19.

Washington, B. B., "Counseling the Disadvantaged Girl," in Amos and Grambs (Eds.), *Counseling the Disadvantaged Youth*, Englewood Cliffs, New Jersey: Prentice-Hall, 1968, pp. 169–189.

Wechsler, D., "The I.Q. is an Intelligence Test," in Miller, H. L. (Ed.), *Education for the Disadvantaged*, New York: The Free Press, 1967, pp. 72–79.

Weinberg, C., "Sociological Explanations for Student Problems," *Personnel and Guidance Journal*, 1968, 46, 855–859.

Welter, P. R., "Case Study: Summer Counseling With Disadvantaged Junior High School Students," *Personnel and Guidance Journal*, 1968, 46, 884–888.

Wiley, R., "Room for Miracles," *American Education*, 1969, 5 (7) 7–10.

INDEX

....